GERMAN THEATRE TODAY

Theatre Today Series also includes:

Disrupting the Spectacle:
Five Years of Experimental and Fringe Theatre in Britain
Peter Ansorge

Playwrights' Theatre: The English Stage Company at the Royal Court
Terry Browne

American Playwrights 1945–75
Catharine Hughes

African Theatre Today
Martin Banham

French Theatre Today
Garry O'Connor

Anger and Detachment:
A Study of Arden, Osborne and Pinter
Michael Anderson

GERMAN THEATRE TODAY

Post-war Theatre in West and East Germany, Austria and Northern Switzerland

Michael Patterson

Pitman Publishing

First published 1976

Pitman Publishing Ltd
Pitman House, 39 Parker Street, London WC2B 5PB, UK

Pitman Medical Publishing Co Ltd
42 Camden Road, Tunbridge Wells, Kent TN1 2QD, UK

Focal Press Ltd
31 Fitzroy Square, London W1P 6BH, UK

Pitman Publishing Corporation
6 East 43 Street, New York, NY 10017, USA

Fearon Publishers Inc
6 Davis Drive, Belmont, California 94002, USA

Pitman Publishing Pty Ltd
Pitman House, 158 Bouverie Street, Carlton, Victoria 3053,
Australia

Pitman Publishing
Copp Clark Publishing
517 Wellington Street West, Toronto M5V 1G1, Canada

Sir Isaac Pitman and Sons Ltd
Banda Street, PO Box 46038, Nairobi, Kenya

Pitman Publishing Co SA (Pty) Ltd
Craighall Mews, Jan Smuts Avenue, Craighall Park,
Johannesburg 2001, South Africa

Cased Edition ISBN 0 273 00350 X
Paperback Edition ISBN 0 273 00293 7

Text set in 10/11 pt. Photon Times, printed by photolithography,
and bound in Great Britain at The Pitman Press, Bath

G.3541/3533:15

To Dixi

Preface

The title *German Theatre Today* requires some clarification. 'German' means here 'German-language' and therefore includes all of Germany, Austria and the German-speaking areas of Switzerland. At the risk of offending any Swiss or Austrian readers, I shall consistently use 'German' in this sense. Where 'German' is intended to define national boundaries, I use the terms 'West German' and 'East German' in preference to the cumbersome designations 'The Federal Republic of Germany' and 'The German Democratic Republic'. 'Theatre' describes both places of performance and what is written for them. I have confined myself to what the Germans call *Sprechtheater* ('speech-theatre', our 'legitimate' theatre) and have ignored *Musiktheater* ('music-theatre': operas, operettas, musicals and ballets), although the two stand much closer to each other than is the case in Britain, often alternating night by night on the same stage. I have also made no more than a passing mention of the 'fringe' theatre, which is especially active in Munich and Berlin. Finally, 'Today' extends back to the day before yesterday and covers the whole post-war period, although relatively more attention has been devoted to the theatre and playwrights of the last ten years.

In the case of play-titles I have used the standard English translation even where I have felt this to be inelegant or inaccurate. It is followed by the date of composition, where known, and then by details of the world-premiere. All other translations, with a couple of exceptions which I indicate, are my own. This is not because I believe my version always to be an improvement on any existing rendering, but because an actable text for the stage does not always offer the accurate reproduction of the original required by the critic.

Apart from the interest of the subject itself, there are two main justifications for presenting this study: first, there is still too little recognition of the importance of German drama for the theatre of Britain and the world (significantly, this is the first book in English devoted to post-war German drama, and some of Germany's leading contemporary playwrights have had no published translations in English, e.g. Peter Hacks, Tankred Dorst, Franz Xaver Kroetz). Secondly, at a time when theatres in Britain are pressing for more state support, it is beneficial to examine the advantages and drawbacks of a system, like that of Germany, where subsidies have been in operation for many years. In this sense, I hope this study will provide not only information and stimulation but perhaps even a corrective.

Michael Patterson,
September 1975

Acknowledgements

Grateful acknowledgement is due to the following for permission to use copyright material:

Verlag der Arche, Peter Schifferli, Zürich; Aufbauverlag, East Berlin; Calder & Boyars, Ltd., London; Europäische Verlagsanstalt, Frankfurt/Main; Friedrich Verlag, Velber bei Hannover; Henschelverlag, East Berlin; Langen-Müller Verlag, Munich; MacGibbon & Kee, Granada Publishing, London; Manchester University Press, Manchester; Methuen & Co., London; Rowohlt Verlag, Reinbek bei Hamburg; Martin Secker & Warburg, Ltd., London; Times Newspapers, Ltd., London; University of Texas Press, Austin, Texas; Volkstheater, Rostock; Oswald Wolff, Ltd., London.

My thanks go to Hugh Rorrison of Leeds University, to Bernhard Scheller of the Karl Marx University, Leipzig, and to all those who have helped me in the writing of this book.

Contents

Preface   vii

1   **Not One Theatre, But Many**
Major Trends in Post-War German Playwriting   1

2   **The Theatre Scene in Germany**   5

3   **The Theatre of History and Myth**
Fritz Hochwälder, Leopold Ahlsen. Hans Henny Jahnn and others   16

4   **The Theatre of Parody and the Grotesque**
Friedrich Dürrenmatt, Wolfgang Hildesheimer and Peter Handke   21

5   **The Theatre That Came to Terms with the Past**
Max Frisch, Wolfgang Borchert, Carl Zuckmayer and Martin Walser   34

6   **Political Theatre in the East**
Bertolt Brecht and the Berliner Ensemble, Peter Hacks, Heiner Müller, and the Theatre Scene in East Germany   45

7   **Political Theatre in the West**
Hartmut Lange, Siegfried Lenz, Peter Weiss, Günter Grass, and Tankred Dorst   64

8   **The Theatre of Fact—Documentary Drama**
Rolf Hochhuth, Heinar Kipphardt, Peter Weiss, Hans Magnus Enzensberger, Dieter Forte and others   75

9   **The Theatre of the Common Man—the Volksstück**
Jochen Ziem, Martin Sperr, Wolfgang Bauer, Franz Xaver Kroetz, Rainer Werner Fassbinder, Heinrich Henkel, Ulrich Plenzdorf and others   88

10   **Conclusion**
The Contribution of Germany to World Theatre Today   101

Chart of Important Productions 1944–75   106

Most frequently produced plays and playwrights 1964–74   114

Short bibliography   118

Index   120

1 Not One Theatre, But Many: Major Trends in Post-War German Playwriting

You see, the dream is very strange. I'll tell it to you. You are listening, aren't you, sir? There's a man and he plays a xylophone. He plays a frenzied rhythm. And he sweats, this man, because he's extraordinarily fat. And he plays on a giant xylophone. And because it's so big, he has to rush up and down in front of the xylophone to hit the different notes. And he sweats, for he really is very fat. But he doesn't sweat sweat, that's what strange. He sweats blood, dark steaming blood. And the blood runs down his trousers in two broad red stripes, so that from a distance he looks like a general. Like a general! A fat, blood-stained general. He must be an old war-veteran, because he has lost both arms. Yes, he plays with long, thin artificial limbs that look like hand-grenades, wooden and with a metal ring. He must be quite an odd musician, this general, because the wooden keys of his huge xylophone are not made of wood. No, believe me, sir, believe me, they're made of bones. Believe me, sir, bones.[1]

Wolfgang Borchert: *Draussen vor der Tür*

In the summer of 1944 I saw the first
of these mutilated corpses
A man was unloaded
whom I had noticed
as he undressed for his execution
He was a giant
I saw him later lying in the wash-room
There were men in white coats
with surgeon's knives
Flesh had been cut
out of his stomach
At first we thought
he had swallowed something
and they had got it back
but afterwards it happened more often
that flesh was taken from the corpses
Later it happened mainly
with well-built women[2]

Peter Weiss: *Die Ermittlung*

1

Stalingrad and Auschwitz. These names celebrate the dual horror of the recent German past—the devastation of war and the atrocities of Fascism.

It would be hard to say when the war ended in Germany and when peace broke out. The date of capitulation, 8 May 1945, meant only the end of hostilities, for German soil was still totally occupied by foreign troops. Indeed, as no formal peace treaty has ever been signed, the Allies are to this day technically still at war with Germany. In a more immediate sense, the war was by no means over for the mass of surviving Germans: there was a dire shortage of food, many cities were little more than rubble and soldiers continued to return home from foreign captivity well into the fifties.

The war for men's minds also continued unabated. The revulsion against war went hand in hand with a revulsion against the ideology that had brought it about. The 'Cold War' was soon to turn Germany into a centre of confrontation between the capitalist democracies of the West and the Communist democracies of the East, but for the time being one ideal united both sides—the rejection of Fascist dictatorship.

The conversion from Fascism was accelerated by the genuine shock felt when the truth about the Nazi extermination of the Jews became known. What had at best been dismissed as the lies of Allied propaganda now became the inescapable fact that Germany had carried out the most efficient programme of genocide in human history.

While writers of the victorious allied nations could pour forth novels, plays and films celebrating their war heroes or giving prurient accounts of Nazi atrocities, the Germans were forced into a much more serious examination of their own past. This self-examination was to become no less than obsessive, and ultimately there were calls to replace the 'Bewältigung der Vergangenheit' ('coming to terms with the past') with 'Überwältigung der Befangenheit' ('overcoming the obsession').

Not all playwrights, admittedly, saw their role in helping their society to come to terms with the past. Some looked back instead beyond the sickness and confusion of recent history to more permanent human conflicts as exemplified in historical or mythical situations. In Chapter 3, 'The Theatre of History and Myth', such writers—Hochwälder, Ahlsen, Jahnn and others—will be considered.

Other writers, confronted with horrors of such magnitude and feeling themselves unable to contain them within the confines of a conventional theatre-piece, resorted to parodistic and grotesque depictions of the world about them. Another quotation from Weiss' oratorio about Auschwitz exemplifies the problem:

> We also had a few aspirins
> they were hung up on threads
> Patients with a temperature of less than 100 degrees
> were allowed one lick
> Patients with a temperature over 100 degrees two[3]

Now this is really not very funny, and yet the incongruity between the solicitude with which the rules are drawn up and the barbarousness which has made them necessary is comic. Where the comic spills over into a profoundly disturbing insight, we may speak of the grotesque.

And it is grotesque comedy which becomes one of the most important styles of post-war theatre—in German-speaking nations as in others; indeed, for its chief exponent, Dürrenmatt, it is the only viable form of contemporary theatre. Together with Dürrenmatt in Chapter 4, 'The Theatre of Parody and the Grotesque', we shall encounter the most popular German absurdist playwright, Wolfgang Hildesheimer, and Peter Handke, who though pursuing a very different line from Dürrenmatt, is, like him, committed to serious statement through comedy and to a position which seeks the worth of man in his rejection of society rather than in his adoption of a social role.

Many writers, however, were concerned with 'coming to terms with the past', some as flagellants, some as apologists, all with an urgent desire to find explanations for the insanity that had swept through the German people. In Chapter 5, 'The Theatre that Came to Terms with the Past', attention is directed towards such playwrights, notably Frisch, Borchert, Zuckmayer and Walser.

As the giant of the past was gradually being reduced to manageable proportions, so there grew a greater concern with the present. The lead here came above all from East Germany, probably because their more radical denazification programme had rapidly relegated Fascism to a thing of the past, certainly also because of the influence of Brecht in East Berlin with his insistence that the theatre must be politically relevant. In Chapter 6, 'Political Theatre in the East', we trace the development of theatre in the German Democratic Republic, the work of Brecht and of his successors, especially Hacks and Müller. Chapter 7 describes 'Political Theatre in the West' with a review of the work of Lange, Lenz, Weiss, Grass and Dorst.

Political theatre is arguably a contradiction in terms. If it attempts to do justice to the complexity of a political situation, theatricality may easily be lost in argument and counter-argument; if it has the clear focus of a good piece of theatre, political problems may be misleadingly simplified. Brecht may have shown the inherently theatrical quality of dialectics, but for many, especially for the Western writers who had no clearly formulated ideology, it seemed increasingly difficult to describe objectively the society in which they lived. One way out of the impasse of confused subjectivity was to base the representation of historical or political themes as closely as possible on fact. In Chapter 8 we shall consider 'The Theatre of Fact'—the documentary drama of Hochhuth, Kipphardt, Weiss, Enzensberger, Forte and others.

When the initial excitement over documentary drama faded away, it was soon recognised for what it is, a bankruptcy of the imagination with no real guarantee of an objective viewpoint. Unable or unwilling to pursue the line of Brechtian political drama, the only way forwards seemed to be backwards—to the *Volksstück*, the naturalistic depiction of everyday scenes of contemporary life, such as had been written by Ödön von Horváth decades previously. Chapter 9, 'The Theatre of the Common Man', shows how much of what is being written in German today, by writers like Ziem, Sperr, Bauer, Kroetz, Henkel and Plenzdorf, is a close-up picture of ordinary citizens. No longer so heavily encumbered by memories of the war or Fascism, living instead in one of the prosperous and stable German-speaking states, these small people have small problems. This, the latest trend in German playwriting, is compassionate without being edifying and offers political implications without political analysis.

In conclusion, Chapter 10 attempts to evaluate the importance of German theatre today for the rest of the world.

Notes to Chapter 1

1. Wolfgang Borchert, *Draussen vor der Tür*, Rowohlt, Reinbek bei Hamburg, 1956, pp. 24–25.
2. Peter Weiss, *Dramen*, Vol. II, Suhrkamp, Frankfurt/Main, 1968, p. 137.
3. Ibid., p. 44.

2 The Theatre Scene in Germany

To the German it is as normal to have a good theatre in his home town as it is for the Englishman to have a public library. And just as the English reader expects to be able to choose any book from Plato to Agatha Christie, so the German theatre-goer demands from his theatre a repertory ranging from Aeschylus to Ayckbourn and from Verdi to Brecht. Where there are theatres in England, the building itself is usually just another in a row of shops, banks and offices. By contrast, German theatres stand in grand isolation from the commercial buildings of the city, 'majestic temples to the Muses'.[1] Since the days of Burbage the English have looked upon their theatres as commercial institutions, it is all "show-*business*", whereas the German tradition derives from the patronage of court-theatres. For them the stage is not so much a source of income as of prestige.

To maintain its claim of being the best-endowed theatre nation in the world (137 standing theatre-companies in 1973), West Germany pays vast amounts in subsidies. It is quite common for a theatre to receive a grant of 10 million Marks a year (almost £2 million p.a.) and in the 1973/74 season the Deutsche Oper in West Berlin received over 32 million Marks (almost £6 million)—a sum not much smaller than the total Arts Council grants to the British theatre. Subsidies represent seldom less than half and usually about three-quarters of the total budget of West German state[2] and municipal theatres. Moreover West Germany is only one part of the German-speaking theatre, for there are excellent and well subsidised theatres in East Germany, Austria and Northern Switzerland. This brings the total number to well over 200, to which may be further added the many studios attached to larger theatres.

This supremacy in the theatre is all the more remarkable when one considers that for a period some thirty years ago not a single German-language theatre was operating outside Switzerland. On 1 September 1944, the Nazis had closed all theatres in Germany and Austria (it is ironical that wartime England, generally far less enthusiastic about its theatre, was encouraging the stage as a boost to morale). The devastation of the last months of the war put a definitive seal on the Nazi ban.

But it seems impossible to suppress the theatre for very long, and it re-emerged almost immediately amongst the ruins of the German cities.

In *The Empty Space* Peter Brook recalls those months after the war:

> In the burnt-out shell of the Hamburg Opera only the stage itself remained—but an audience assembled on it whilst against the back wall on a wafer-thin set singers clambered up and down to perform *The Barber of Seville*, because nothing would stop them doing so. In a tiny attic fifty people crammed together while in the inches of remaining space a handful of the best actors resolutely continued to practise their art. In a ruined Düsseldorf, a minor Offenbach about smugglers and bandits filled the theatre with delight. There was nothing to discuss, nothing to analyse—in Germany that winter, as in London a few years before, the theatre was responding to a hunger.[3]

Before 1945 was over, the Deutsches Theater had reopened in East Berlin, the Schlossparktheater (under Boleslaw Barlog) in West Berlin, and the Burgtheater in Vienna. The Deutsches Theater saw the return of two great men of the theatre: Gustaf Gründgens, who acted and directed there in 1946 until he went to Düsseldorf the following year, and Brecht, returning from exile, who worked at the Deutsches Theater from 1949 to 1954, when he transferred to the Theater am Schiffbauerdamm, still the home of the famous Berliner Ensemble.

Apart from Brecht's specialised work, to which we shall return later, nearly all the re-emergent theatres adopted the programme model which had been established in the war years by the Zurich Schauspielhaus. Heinz Hilpert, later to direct the new Deutsches Theater in Göttingen, recorded his debt to Zurich on the occasion of his premiere of Zuckmayer's *Des Teufels General* (*The Devil's General*) in 1946:

> The Zurich Schauspielhaus has preserved and developed the concept and essence of German theatre in Germany's darkest and most merciless hour and so has enabled us after the great vacuum to find a new point at which we may begin our work in the theatre.[4]

The recipe prescribed in Zurich has been administered fairly constantly in the thirty years since: disregarding opera, ballet, operetta and musicals, which represent over a third of all stage-productions, and setting aside the smaller private theatres which tend to favour light entertainment, the standard mixture is roughly 40% "classics", 25% plays from Ibsen to World War II and 35% serious contemporary drama, of which only some 12% is German. The repertory is usually performed in rotation with a different production each night of the week.

Shakespeare has been the consistently most popular playwright—every fifth classical production is by him and he is performed by at least half the German-language theatres each year. His popularity has been superseded only by Schiller in the Schiller Centenary Year (1959/60 season) and more recently and more surprisingly by Brecht (1967/68 and 1973/74 seasons). As an example of more recent 'classics', Shaw used to be given some 40 different productions a year, and although his popularity is now on the decline, one can confidently claim that he is performed more often in Germany than in England. As for the contemporary scene, it is significant that the world-premiere of Ionesco's *The Rhinoceroses* took place in Düsseldorf and of Pinter's

The Dumb Waiter in Frankfurt, and German audiences are more familiar with writers like Arden and Bond than the English themselves.

All this makes Germany seem a theatre-goer's paradise to the English and American who have to live with commercial theatre and poor subsidies. Thanks too to the luxury of financial security, German theatres can maintain standing companies, usually with three or even five year contracts, and do not have to rely on a turnover of stars to ensure a good box-office. It is a luxury that allowed Gertrud Mander a certain justified superciliousness when she reported in the West German monthly *Theater heute* on the contemporary London scene:

> [The theatre-bills] suppress the names of the author in half of the West End plays; instead of Shaw's name alongside *Captain Brassbound's Conversion*, there appear in big letters before the title the names of Ingrid Bergman, Joss Ackland and Kenneth Williams, who as stars apparently offer a greater attraction to the non-intellectual theatre-goer than G.B.S. If the author happens to be named, then it is in as small print as the actors or even smaller. All of which expresses an important reality of commercial London theatre: it is sustained by the stars, they and the title of the play are the ticket of sale.[5]

By contrast, the German repertory system is not conducive to creating stars. In line with the tradition established by the Duke of Saxe-Meiningen in the last century, it is ideally the case that an actor may be called to fill any role and that his salary will not depend upon his public success. Even if in practice this ideal may be often compromised, it is nevertheless true that few German actors achieve star-billing such as is common in the West End or on Broadway. It is anyway most unlikely that for the sake of one of their own actors Germans would queue all night and defend their places with physical violence, as I witnessed Berliners doing in order to see Olivier play Othello. Hardly any German stage-actors have become internationally famous: some people outside Germany may be familiar with the names of Gustaf Gründgens (1899–1963), perhaps best remembered for his playing of Mephistopheles in his own production of Goethe's *Faust*, which later appeared as a film; Ernst Deutsch (1890–1969), famed for his classical roles; Tilla Durieux (1880–1971) still performing until a few years ago despite her great age; O. E. Hasse (b. 1903), who in 1973 was still capable of receiving one critic's nomination for the best performance of the year; and Martin Held (b. 1908), whose most notable recent success was his presentation of *Krapp's Last Tape* under the direction of Beckett in 1969. The names of two leading performers of the Berliner Ensemble, Ernst Busch (b. 1900) and Helene Weigel (1900–1972), Brecht's wife, may be known, but all these actors are either dead or well advanced in years, and the younger generation of German actors (like Jutta Lampe or Bruno Ganz) is certainly unknown outside Germany and often even outside their own theatres.

When one thinks of the best of German acting, one thinks less of individual contributions than of the strong quality of ensemble playing. It is symptomatic that the 1971 Schaubühne am Halleschen Ufer production of *Peer Gynt* made use of six actors to play the title-role, and one recalls that, however divergent their styles were, both Piscator and

Reinhardt devoted more attention to an integrated performance by the company as a whole than to creating pieces in which the stars might shine. It follows that from the demands of ensemble playing the general style of German acting is more disciplined and less individualistic than it is in Britain.

This discipline extends also to the diction of actors: because of its peculiar situation in having no cultural capital and no standard pronunciation, Germany has created a super-regional *Bühnensprache* (stage-language), which is basically High German with a few added affectations like a very strongly rolled uvular 'r'. As Leroy R. Shaw once remarked:

> ... on the stage, as on the street, High German is more an act of will than of impulse, an instrument of achievement rather than a source of renewal.[6]

Well suited for classics, *Bühnensprache* can give a ring of artificiality to Naturalist plays. Such plays will therefore often be performed in dialect, thus rendering them incomprehensible—or at best faintly ludicrous—to German speakers from other areas. (A Berlin audience treated Wolfgang Bauer's serious piece *Change* as a huge joke when it was played there in Viennese accents in 1969.)

Another effect of the repertory system is to encourage adaptability in acting styles. It is expected of the German actor that he will move from a Stanislavskian mode to a Brechtian approach as the production demands; whereas I share Albert Hunt's opinion that in Britain there is no group of professional actors who can cope with the playing of a Brecht piece, except perhaps fringe groups like the Half Moon Theatre or the Joint Stock Company. But what the British actor does well, he tends to do very well, while his German counterpart seldom has the opportunity to specialise in a particular style of performance or to exhaust the possibilities of a single role. Donald Wolfit may have defended his ability to play several roles in a week of repertory by saying that you don't take your golf-clubs when you want to play tennis, but it is still a very tall order for an actor to perform in Sophocles one night, Ibsen the following and Beckett the next. The tennis racquet and the golf-clubs tend to be replaced by an all-purpose hitting stick.

If there are any stars in the German theatre, then they are the directors. Helped by the facts that Germany has no theatre-capital and that German theatre-critics do not share their British counterparts' aversion to travel, it is possible for an *Intendant* (Chief Director) to transform a small provincial stage into a theatre-centre. One of the more striking examples of this has been the interest shown in the work of Hans Schalla and more recently Peter Zadek in the industrial town of Bochum, a kind of German Coventry, whose company participated in the Aldwych World Theatre Season in 1973.

Such transformations tend to be the exception, however, and the leading directors are usually associated with the traditional theatre-centres: we have already mentioned Bert Brecht in East Berlin and Boleslaw Barlog (b. 1906) in West Berlin, *Intendant* of the Schillertheater from its opening in 1951 until his retirement in 1970; Gustaf Gründgens (1899–1963), who became *Intendant* of the Deutsches Schauspielhaus in Hamburg in 1955 after being succeeded in Düsseldorf by the former Schillertheater director, Karl Heinz Stroux (b. 1908); and Heinz Hilpert (1890–1964), *Intendant* of the new Deutsches Theater in Göttingen from 1950. To these names should be added others, like that of Erwin Piscator, the great innovator of the twenties, who after many frustrating years on returning from exile was finally given his own theatre, the Freie Volksbühne in West Berlin, where he worked from 1962 until his death four years later. Then there is the director responsible for some of the earliest Brecht productions in Western Germany, Harry Buckwitz (b. 1904). He left the Munich Kammerspiele in 1950 to direct the municipal theatre in Frankfurt until 1968. Then after a period of free-lance work including visits to the USA, he became *Intendant* of the Zurich Schauspielhaus. Hans Schweikart (b. 1895) is known mainly for his work with the Munich Kammerspiele. Finally, Fritz Kortner (1892–1970), one of the most honoured of the older generation of directors, is owed a large debt for curing his actors of the declamatory bad habits of the Nazi period[7] and so opening the way to new and more subtle interpretations of the classics.

In the wake of the political upheavals of 1968, many theatre companies unseated or at least attempted to unseat the older and all-powerful *Intendanten* and tried to establish a system of participation in which all would have a say in the running of the theatre and so reduce the *Indendant* to a democractically elected *primus inter pares*. It is in circumstances like these that one of the major disadvantages of subsidies becomes apparent. Although they have shown themselves to be reasonably tolerant about the plays they help to finance, many state and municipal authorities in the West have repeatedly expressed their dissatisfaction with the 'subversive' tendencies of more progressive theatres. One of the unhappiest examples has been the relationship between the town of Basle and its theatre. It has culminated in the recent fracas surrounding the appointment of a new *Intendant*. The left-wing director, Arno Wüstenhöfer, had been called from Wuppertal to take up the post, but when it was learned that he intended to open the season with a political piece directed by the East German Ruth Berghaus, his appointment was not confirmed. Meanwhile in Wuppertal the authorities are breathing a sigh of relief as they look forward to a more balanced and digestible diet of plays under their new *Intendant*.

On the question of participation most theatre managements, themselves not free to act independently, proved unable or unwilling to meet the challenge. This is borne out by their replies to a questionnaire in *Theater 1970*: 'have anyway always worked as a team', 'no representation on questions of casting or the administration itself', 'Tendencies towards participation by the ensemble do not exist'.[8] The few exceptions, where a genuinely democratic administration came into being, could usually be distinguished by their adoption of initials, as the LTT—Landestheater Tübingen—or the TAT—Theater-am-Turm, Frankfurt, which carried out some important experimental work, including the premieres of many Handke pieces.

More significant than the only partially successful attempts at participation was the rise to prominence after 1968 of a number of younger and more inventive directors: Werner Düggelin in Basle, Peter Palitzsch in Frankfurt, Hansgünther Heyme in Cologne, Peter Zadek in Bochum and Peter Stein in Bremen and at the Schaubühne am Halleschen Ufer, West Berlin.

It is even harder to generalise about directing styles than it is about acting. There is tremendous diversity—from the traditional and rather operatic productions at the Burgtheater in Vienna to the Brechtian austerity of Heyme's work in Cologne. There has never been a strong tradition in German theatre, which helps to explain why Germany has always been so receptive to world-theatre and why it has been a breeding-ground of radical experimentation—from the Storm and Stress movement in the eighteenth century to Expressionism, Piscator and Brecht in this. What tradition there might have been was anyway swept aside when the new generation of post-war directors rejected the Wagnerian style of the Nazi period.

Inasmuch as it is possible to generalise about contemporary German directing styles, three points may be made. First, directors tend towards the economy of Brecht rather than the detail of Naturalism or the ritual of Artaud. Even in fairly conventional productions, sets are usually evocative rather than realistic, as exemplified in the work of outstanding designers like Caspar Neher, Karl von Appen or Wilfried Minks. Given the vast stage of the typical German playhouse, minimal sets are almost essential so as not to dwarf the actor. The resultant impression is generally one of great spaciousness, allowing and indeed necessitating long moves by the actors. As with acting styles, direction tends to be tight and disciplined and well-informed, taking account of the background to the play and often inviting a critical stance towards it. Some directors, like Peter Stein, will even arrange talks to his actors on the social and political context of the play they are rehearsing. One of these was a lecture on the structure of nineteenth-century society in France as part of their work on a farce by Labiche! It is generally fair to say that meaning takes precedence over theatricality and information over entertainment.

From this follows the second point that German directors are not at their best when handling comedy. (One may recall Harold Pinter's bewilderment at the deep solemnity with which the premiere of *The Dumb Waiter* was played and received in Frankfurt). It would be too easy to write this off as a reflection of Teutonic humourlessness, but it is undeniable that there is no strong comic tradition on the German stage. It is my personal conviction too that a Brechtian style, though greatly entertaining, does not make for lighthearted laughter. The Brechtian performer is required to maintain a consistently critical attitude towards his role, but it is common experience that there is little so unfunny as a comic who is self-conscious about his humour. I remember Ekkehard Schall in the title-role of the Berliner Ensemble production of Brecht's *Arturo Ui* presenting the potentially hilarious scene in which the Hitler-figure Ui is practising impressive poses with a teacher of rhetoric. The stage-business was calculated, grotesque, perfectly timed and made a powerful comment on the Hitler charisma, but it simply was not very funny. The politics was sound, but I laughed inside my head only.

Thirdly, there is a great premium placed on originality. This is understandable in a theatrical situation where any director faced with the prospect of producing, say, Schiller's *Don Carlos*,[9] cannot ignore the fact that it has been seen in several hundred different productions since the war. Naturally, often as not, he will attempt to do something new with it. At its best this produces new insights into the classic (in the manner of Peter Brook's *A Midsummer Night's Dream*); at its worst we have self-indulgent spectacle obscuring the original. As one actress put it, 'When I go to see *Maria Stuart*, I want to see the play by Schiller and not watch two girls on roller-skates.'[10]

The first step may well be to invite a writer to adapt the original text (Brecht's influence at work again!). *Theater 1972* commented ironically: 'We cannot expect a progressive public to come to [Shakespeare's] plays unless they have been adapted; that's what the tax-payer pays his subsidies for.'[11] Thereafter inventiveness is given free rein. Two of the most striking recent productions of classics have been Peter Zadek's version of *King Lear* in Bochum and the Schaubühne production of Euripides' *Bacchae*, directed by Klaus Michael Grüber, both in 1974. Interestingly enough, neither was performed in a theatre, *King Lear* being staged in a cinema and *The Bacchae* in an exhibition hall, a reflection of the frustration felt by young directors at the unrelieved conventionality of nearly all German theatre architecture. Despite a vast programme of new theatre building and reconstruction, West Germany has only one truly flexible auditorium—the Podiumtheater in Ulm—and that is a mere 200-seater.[12] Nor was either production typical of German style, since the one clearly belonged to what Peter Brook calls 'Rough Theatre' and the other might be fairly classified as 'Theatre of Cruelty'.

In his approach to *Lear* Zadek[13] confessed himself influenced by American vaudeville, Buster Keaton and the Marx Brothers. He invited the actor playing Gloster to study the technique of W. C. Fields and used a circus setting as a starting-point. Work on the production lasted four months, usually with rehearsals in the morning and lengthy discussions with the cast in the evenings. Almost nothing was decided in advance: a variety of props and costumes would be brought up from the store. The cast were encouraged to choose their own and then try out different and extravagant ways of playing their roles. When it was felt that something was not working, the group tried to analyse the reason. This improvisational approach lasted until two or three weeks before the opening and in some respects even continued into the performance. Some of the effects achieved were as brilliant as they were simple: Gloster's blinding was represented by ramming his top-hat (*sic*) down over his eyes, and his 'fall' over the cliff was realised by Edgar snapping his stick in two, so that he felt his way with half a stick and thus imagined himself at a precipice. The deaths were carried out with gruesome exaggeration: blood poured from twisted mouths, limbs were torn off, Regan drowned flailing in a barrel. All this was done to throw the death of Cordelia into relief: her body was carried on naked, slung over Lear's shoulder. The *Grand Guignol* of the preceding deaths made the simplicity of this scene intensely meaningful.

In comparison, the Schaubühne *Bacchae* was quite elaborately staged. Horses were brought on and dogs that devoured meat. Much of the text was recited in Ancient Greek or chanted unintelligibly. Dionysos was wheeled on to a blindingly white stage on an operating-trolley. Agaue after murdering her son was drenched in blood that dropped from her in heavy clots. These are just a few impressions of productions that would be virtually unthinkable experiments in the commercial theatre of Britain.

If they are almost unthinkable in Britain, then it is only fair to admit that they are exceptional for Germany. A much more typical offering would be a recent production I saw at the Schiller-Theater in Berlin. It was of Hartmut Lange's *Die Gräfin von Rathenow* (*The Countess of Rathenow*) and was directed by the author himself. For someone like myself coming from a working situation where 'Poor Theatre' is as much an economic necessity as an aesthetic goal, the dressing of this production seemed overwhelmingly luxurious. Extensive use was made of the revolving stage, huge buildings slid into place almost noiselessly, carriages powered by electric motors circled the stage. The play is a tightly, lightly written piece and demands an appropriately simple treatment. There was no clutter, but the technical bag of tricks obscured the clear line of the plot. Interested to know why the author/director and his designer had made use of so much stage machinery, I was told that it had not been part of their original conception. A certain sum of money had been allocated to the production and this had to be spent. Sadly this is a not untypical example of the neat circle in which subsidies are spent to justify subsidies.

The actors and their direction were flawless. The groupings were perfectly arranged, the timing, especially of pauses, could not have been better. Only: I had the feeling that the groupings would always assume those perfect arrangements, that every time the play was staged those pauses would remain the same length to the fraction of a second. Nothing, it seemed, would disturb the smooth running of this machine, would give it the true spontaneity of a *live* performance. In short, I was bored.

So when we in Britain despair over our commercial theatre and long for more state subsidy, we should be aware of the dangers. The British theatre may be like a prostitute selling herself on the street-corner, but she is perhaps preferable to Germany's staid matron who will often perform only from a sense of marital duty.

A powerful ally of the director in his work—for better or worse—is the *Dramaturg*. This post, for which the only equivalent in England is the Literary Manager at the National Theatre, is normally occupied by someone with a good academic background and training in the theatre. His functions include script-reading and recommendations for works to be taken up into the repertory, full research into the historical and theatrical background of each piece, possibly supervision of translation or adaptation, collaboration with the director during rehearsal—often acting as a kind of front-line critic—writing extensive programme notes and collating critics' and audience response with the possibility of recommending certain changes in performance. Some of the major modern German playwrights—Brecht, Zuckmayer, Kipphardt and Hacks among them—worked as *Dramaturg*.

Despite the useful assistance of the *Dramaturg*, it is nevertheless the case that few German theatres fully satisfy the high demands made on them by the repertory system, and it is significant that work of consistently high quality has normally only been produced by theatres which specialise in one style like the Berliner Ensemble or strictly limit their output like the Schaubühne am Halleschen Ufer.

The Schaubühne is often regarded as what German theatre should be. It was formed in 1962 and managed to survive without subsidies for some years. It is not a purpose-built theatre, being a hall rented from a Trades Union organisation. This lends some freedom in staging but adds considerably to the cost of sets—even a relatively straightforward set costs some 40,000 DM (app. £7,500). From 1970 it has been based on strong communal principles and all decisions are reached by the ensemble as a whole. Despite mutterings about the subversive left-wing character of their work, the Schaubühne now receives generous subsidies from the West Berlin Senate, money which it devotes to a limited number of well thought-out productions in preference to the more usual pattern of presenting some eighteen different pieces in an annual season.

While the wide range of theatres obviously promotes writing for the stage, the young German author finds much to complain about. Since the subsidised theatres operate as museums of classical and contemporary dramatic literature from all over the world, serious contemporary German plays occupy only one eighth of the complete programme. Living writers can count themselves fortunate with even this small allocation, for the public would see it further reduced. No national survey of public taste has been carried out, but the poll taken by the Städtische Bühnen Frankfurt in November 1970 seems representative. While those asked were satisfied with the 40% classical element, they were in favour of only 25% contemporary plays, and in the nomination for preferred authors, living German playwrights like Grass, Hochhuth and Handke came at the end of the list, polling about 1% each.

The explanation for this conservatism in public taste lies in the composition of the audience. *Theater 1971* summarised the situation as follows:

> Where [theatres] can produce the results of polls—whether home-made or carried out with the help of institutes—they all point towards the already known and often lamented fact, a fact that could be learnt any evening by casting a … glance into the stalls of any municipal theatre, namely that—judging by the manner of speech, dress and general behaviour—it is above all the representatives of the cultured middle-classes which occupy the seats that are not empty; and that—judging by the many heads of white hair—the public is hopelessly aged.[14]

Going to the theatre is still primarily a social activity for the average German couple; even in Socialist East Germany he will wear his suit, she will wear her long dress. In the interval they will leave their seats, not to rush for the bar but to promenade together amongst the other theatre-goers. Like as not, they will have come to this particular production not by choice but because they are season-ticket holders, perhaps members of the '*Volksbühne*'. This 'People's Stage' was founded in Berlin in 1890 and was soon imitated in many other cities. In 1933 it was absorbed into the Nazi *Deutsche Bühne* but reconstituted in West Germany after the war. It now has some half a million members. Originally conceived as a means of providing a varied theatrical diet for the workers, it is now almost entirely a middle-class institution (compare the similar development of the Workers' Educational Association in Britain). Peter Zadek has done his utmost to attract the workers of Bochum into his theatre and—on his own reckoning—has succeeded in raising the proletarian element of his audience to 1%! Although season-ticket holders courageously attend quite experimental and even subversive plays, so contributing in great measure to the financial health of German theatre, such plays merely seem to reinforce the conservatism of their taste. In 1969 the *Intendant* of the Württembergische Landesbühne reported:

> In every town of our area a split in the public may be clearly seen. On the one hand there are the season-ticket holders of long standing and the Cultural Committee who choose the plays for their towns. On the other hand there are extremely critical young people. This often leads to virtually schizophrenic situations, e.g. a play is very well received by a young audience, but is nevertheless accounted a failure by those in positions of responsibility, who explain that this kind of theatre reinforces anarchistic tendencies. In our experience every theatre at the moment has to come to terms with this situation.'[15]

Not only does the contemporary German playwright have to combat his public's lack of enthusiasm for new work, but his financial situation is precarious. He receives 10% of the box-office, which sounds generous enough until one remembers that the box-office takings may represent only a quarter of the theatre's income. The writer sees nothing of the subsidies. Nowadays the tendency is more and more towards performing new works in small studio-theatres, where the audiences and consequently the writer's rewards are limited. Asked in 1972 whether they could live from writing plays, only three of thirteen leading young German playwrights answered with a definite yes, and at least one of those depends on income from television performances of his work.[16]

The lack of a theatre capital also works both for and against the playwright. To have so many major provincial theatres in rivalry with one another provides much greater opportunities than are offered to English-language writers who must look to the West End or Broadway for real success. A director of a small theatre in Germany knows that the only way he can initially attract the attention of national critics is to mount a premiere, preferably by an already known author. This is beneficial to the playwright who has already made some name for himself, but it does mean that it is hard to achieve that first step and even harder for the playwright whose first step has been a failure.

The undoubted splendour of the German theatre must not then be allowed to blind us to its imperfections. Germany *is* the leading theatre nation, but this only serves to remind us of the unhealthy state of the theatre in the rest of the world. All is not for the best in the best of all theatrical nations.

Notes to Chapter 2

1. Peter Fischer, 'Doing Princely Sums—Structure and Subsidy' *The German*

14

Theatre, ed. R. Hayman, Oswald Wolff, London, 1975, p. 219. This article provides a good account of the history and practice of subsidies in German theatre.

2. 'State' here refers to the Federal States or *Länder* of West Germany. There has never been centralised state supervision or support of the theatre, except in the Third Reich when it fell under the jurisdiction of Goebbels' Ministry of Propaganda. A fuller discussion of theatre in East Germany will come in Chapter 6 on political theatre in the East.

3. Peter Brook, *The Empty Space*, Penguin Books, Harmondsworth, 1972, p. 49, (originally published by MacGibbon & Kee).

4. Programme-note for Carl Zuckmayer's *Des Teufels General*, Zurich Schauspielhaus, 14 December, 1946.

5. *Theater 1971*, Friedrich Verlag, Velber, 1971, p. 90.

6. *The German Theatre Today*, ed. Leroy R. Shaw, University of Texas Press, Austin, 1963, p. 4.

7. 'The lines were declaimed stiffly, ending with an outburst like a soldier reporting a message. Of course they had gestures: gestures with which they seized the fake sword that hung invisible on their belts'. Fritz Kortner, cit. *Theatre 1970*, Friedrich Verlag, Velber, 1970, p. 46.

8. *Theater 1970*, pp. 109ff.

9. It says a great deal about the comparative nature of British and German theatre to reflect that *Don Carlos*, one of the major German classics, had to wait almost two hundred years, until 1975, for its professional premiere in Britain!

10. *Theater 1974*, p. 12.

11. *Theater 1972*, p. 58.

12. For further information on contemporary German theatre architecture, see Klaus Völker, 'The New Theatre Buildings', *The German Theatre*, ed. R. Hayman, Oswald Wolff, London, 1975, pp. 235–246.

13. Peter Zadek (b. 1926) is one of the most provocative of Germany's young directors. Interestingly, he began his career in the English Theatre and seeks above all to entertain his audiences. This does not mean that he has nothing to say, however: his *Merchant of Venice* with a thoroughly repulsive Shylock and his version of Dorst's *Eiszeit (Ice-Age)* with a likeable old Nazi were intended as serious challenges to the uncritical prejudices of post-war Germans.

14. *Theater 1971*, p. 126.

15. *Theater 1969*, p. 115.

16. *Theater 1972*, pp. 84–85.

3 The Theatre of History and Myth

There is a useful word in German, *Epigonen*, literally meaning those who are born after. It is used to describe writers who are not innovators but who follow in the steps of an established tradition. The *Epigonen* of the contemporary German theatre retreated from the confusions of the present to the sure ground of myth and to the ethical conflicts of Schillerian historical drama.

The most successful of these has been the Catholic Austrian playwright Fritz Hochwälder, whose well-made plays have found continuing favour with the German theatre-going public. Born in Vienna in 1911, he worked as a master-upholsterer until 1938, when after the *Anschluss* he illegally fled to Switzerland. Prevented from practising his trade, he devoted himself to his hobby of playwriting. He still lives and writes in Zurich, a man at odds with the world about him. He believes it to be in a state of decline, a fact which he claims is reflected in the bad theatre being created at present:

> When you consider that we live . . . in a time of decay, . . . then it is not surprising that amongst others the art of drama is in decline. What is surprising is that contemporary manufacturers of theatrical rubbish consider themselves original and progressive. That is something their Roman forbears would never have imagined.[1]

Hochwälder's disillusionment with contemporary theatre and his turning back to the firm tradition of the *pièce bien faite* are reflected in his insistence on describing himself as a master-craftsman, despite the fact that he was forced to abandon his trade almost forty years ago. The strength of his work lies in the sheer technical competence with which he tells his dramatic stories, as revealed in his first success and best-known play, *Das heilige Experiment* (*The Strong are Lonely*, 1942). It relates how Spanish power-politics bring about the end of a virtually Utopian native settlement led by Jesuits in Paraguay in the eighteenth century. Premiered in Switzerland in 1943, it achieved international acclaim after its production in Paris in 1952 and its subsequent success in London and New York.

His two major post-war plays are *Der öffentliche Ankläger* (*The Public Prosecutor*, 1948, premiere 1948 Neuss Theater Stuttgart) and

Donadieu (1953, premiere 1953 Burgtheater Vienna). The latter, based on a ballad by the Swiss poet Meyer, is set in France in 1629, when the precarious peace established by the Edict of Nantes had been disrupted by battles between Huguenots and the Crown. To the Huguenot castle of Donadieu come two emissaries from the King, seeking hospitality on their way to proclaim a new royal edict guaranteeing the Protestants freedom of worship in return for total surrender. In the First Act it is established that one of the emissaries had committed an atrocity in this very house, murdering Donadieu's wife before the eyes of their daughter. Act Two shows Donadieu struggling between his desire for revenge and the need to submit himself for the sake of the promised freedom of worship for his fellow-believers. In Act Three, having resolved to accept humiliation at the hands of his wife's murderer, he is driven to almost inhuman limits by the man's taunts. He is suddenly and unexpectedly avenged by the other royal emissary, who justifies killing his companion with the words: 'To do justice means: to cleanse yourself of your own evil'.[2]

The plot unfolds by means of melodramatic discoveries and sudden peripeteiae. The discovery of the murderer, Du Bosc, by the daughter, Judith, is a good example of Hochwälder's method. Du Bosc, feverish and yet already vaguely aware of what house he is in, has been sitting in the dim light of the fire. Judith now brings him a jug of some potion to help his fever:

Du Bosc drops his hat and cloak on to the chair, slowly approaches the table, moves into the light of the candles. Judith stiffens as she sees his face for the first time. Du Bosc reaches out his hand to take the jug. Judith places the jug on the table without taking her eyes off Du Bosc.

DU BOSC (*agitatedly*) You're looking—

Pause

DU BOSC What's the matter?—What—are you looking at?— What?—I'm a human being!—A human being!—Don't you know what a human being looks like?

Judith remains unchanged

DU BOSC (*already withdrawing into the darkness*)—I don't know you! —I've never seen you before!—I've never been here—never —(*He can no longer speak and is now quite lost to sight.*)[3]

This is a typically rewarding scene for actors: there is no complexity of emotion, but simply a nice contrast between the shocked immobility of the girl and the stammering guilt of Du Bosc. The tension is developed by the use of lighting and of gesture (the "unveiling" as he drops hat and cloak, the composure with which Judith sets down the jug in place of the more predictable but theatrically less effective possibility that she might drop it). We feel ourselves in the presence of a theatrical craftsman, someone who can handle well the mechanics of the play, the exposition and development and the climaxes like this one.

When we consider the implications of the play, however, we find that its arresting moments do not add up to very much. Is Donadieu right to swallow down his revenge, is some divine vindication to be seen in the killing of Du Bosc by his fellow emissary? Are we to view Donadieu's inactivity in the historical perspective of the later persecution of the Huguenots? Do we care anyway? Frankly not much; this is the kind of play whose technical skill will give an immediate and superficial satisfaction in the theatre (which is more than can be said of many plays!), but which does not send the audience out into the night with any new thoughts about themselves or the society in which they live. And this is no doubt the key to Hochwälder's continuing popularity.

His other major play, *Der öffentliche Ankläger*, also deals with atrocities, this time those legalised by the courts of the French Revolution. Fouquier-Tinville, the Public Prosecutor, has managed to stay in office through all the turbulence and guillotinings of the Revolution but has now outlived his usefulness, as the Reign of Terror is past. He is, however, so powerful—a mighty and incorruptible functionary of the law unaffected by political change—that his position seems unassailable. Tallien, the leader of the Thermidor, conceives the clever plan of allowing Fouquier to conduct the prosecution with his usual ruthlessness against an unnamed party. When all the preparations for this one final guillotining are irrevocably laid down and the trial has been successfully conducted, Fouquier will be presented with a death-certificate bearing his own name.

There is enough tingling irony in this situation alone to support an exciting plot, but Hochwälder goes further. Theresia, the wife of Tallien, has reasons enough to wish her husband out of the way, reasons known to Fouquier. Moreover, it is she who sets the name on the death-certificate. So the audience (and indeed Tallien himself) are left in real suspense until the name is actually read out.

In a play written two years after the end of the war it is impossible to ignore the relevance of Fouquier's situation to that of former Nazi judges, especially when he defends himself by saying: 'I merely used the means put into my hands. I deny any responsibility![4] Hochwälder can hardly have been unaware of the questions he was touching upon, but we may search in vain for answers or analysis. Once again the dramatic quality is exhausted in momentary theatrical excitement.

Not even as much may be said for another play centred on a historical conflict, Reinhold Schneider's *Der grosse Verzicht* (*The Great Renunciation*, 1949–50, premiere 1958 in Bregenz by the Ensemble of the Burgtheater Vienna). In long-winded prose scenes the play tells the story of the venerable hermit Petrus of Murrhone who was elected Pope in the thirteenth century but who renounced the office when he found himself unable to reconcile the political machinations of the Papacy with the true spirit of the gospel. In the tradition of Schillerian historical drama Schneider hoped to discover in this situation an image which would 'represent the meaning of an era in its relationship to eternity'. What for Schiller was a significant undertaking in the period of German classicism, however, now seemed in these post-war years remote and escapist.

Similarly remote were the attempts by *Epigonen* to escape into the world of myth. Brecht in his *Antigone* and Peter Hacks in his Greek dramas have shown that the modern treatment of myth can be relevant to the concerns of an audience today, but as with Hochwälder's and Schneider's use of historical themes many contemporary versions of myth subscribe to a vague humanism which in its attempt to be relevant for all time is ultimately relevant to none. The pattern had already been set by the aging Gerhart Hauptmann who in his gloomy reworking of the Atridean myth (*Die Atriden-Tetralogie*, 1940–44 premiere 1962, Freie Volksbühne Berlin directed by Piscator) showed Iphigeneia's self-sacrifice at Delphi as the only means of respite from the hideous chain of murder and revenge.

Despite its modern dress, Egon Vietta's *Iphigenie in Amerika* (1948) joins with Hauptmann in 'returning to the recognition of the Ancient Greeks that it is not man who directs history but superhuman forces'.[5] So, although the play is set in modern America, complete with Orestes and Pylades being hunted by a sheriff with tracker-dogs, the author calls on Athene to waft down and solve the confused problems of the mortals.

Other less adventurous post-war treatments of myth succeed better by retaining more of the quality of the original, as in Bernt von Heiseler's *Philoktet* (1947) or Ferdinand Bruckner's *Pyrrhus und Andromache* (1951), closely based on Sophocles and Racine respectively.

On the other hand, the modern playwright may succeed by taking the barest outline from the original myth and using it to treat a contemporary theme. The best example of this process is Leopold Ahlsen's *Philemon und Baukis* (1955, premiere 1956 Kammerspiele, Munich). The myth relates how the old couple offered hospitality to Zeus and Hermes, were rewarded by being saved from a flood and were finally able to spend eternity beside each other by being transformed into an ash and a linden. In Ahlsen's version the old couple shelter a wounded German soldier and are executed by Greek partisans for their 'treachery'—by hanging from an ash and a linden. It is a simple, sentimental well told story which accounts for its popularity both as a stage-play and as a film under the title, *Am Galgen hängt die Liebe* (*Love Hangs on the Gallows*).

Of all the post-war *Epigonen* the most successful product is one based on a historical rather than a mythical theme: Hans Henny Jahnn's *Thomas Chatterton* (1954, premiere 1956 Deutsches Schauspielhaus Hamburg, directed by Gründgens). Jahnn (1894–1959) is probably the most neglected German author of this century. His cranky ideas about biology and the building of pyramids in Europe to be set against the ravages of time, his championing of homosexuality, none of this has helped. It is saddening that he as one of the most inventive minds of late Expressionism is never represented in anthologies and seldom referred to in the critical literature.

His *Thomas Chatterton* retains some elements of his earlier Expressionist writing, notably the episodic structure with the unity being provided by the central character alone. The style too is elevated and poetic, and there is a characteristically Expressionistic *chiaroscuro* effect in the shadowy figure of the angel-traveller, Aburiel.

The first edition of the play in 1955 bore the sub-title 'modelled on historical fact' and Jahnn's version does quite closely follow the actual life of Chatterton in Bristol and London, his sale of forgeries and his eventual suicide. As in history, the suicide is not wholly explained and we are left in some doubt whether Chatterton kills himself from a sense of failure, or because he has contracted syphilis or from a general morbid depression (as his mother says in the First Scene: 'You seem to be made of nothing but death')[6]. The main source of Chatterton's agony is the discovery that the society in which he lives acclaims his forgeries but gives him no recognition as a poet. As Aburiel says in a kind of epilogue addressed to the audience immediately after Chatterton has taken arsenic and opium:

> When an eighteen-year-old who was touched by genius dies as a hungry outcast, the guilty remain behind. The poor who own nothing are acquitted. The rulers, the owners, the masters, who stuff their mouths, may be asked: do you expect a powerless angel who must care for the chosen few, to do deals, to steal, rob, deceive and strike your sort down in order to preserve a valuable life? The duty of angels is different. But it is the duty of men not to incur guilt by neglecting the best amongst you.[7]

Where Hochwälder's ability to move seems exhausted as the final curtain falls, and many of the adapters of myth seek mystical and supernatural solutions to the dramatic conflicts they portray, Jahnn's play issues a challenge to the audience and the angel-figure is not there to provide an easy answer but to throw responsibility squarely back at the audience. Powerful and interesting though *Thomas Chatterton* is, its style looks back to a theatre of the past. The way forward for the post-war German theatre was to lie in very different directions.

Notes to Chapter 3

1. *Theater 1969*, Friedrich, Velber bei Hannover, p. 18.
2. Fritz Hochwälder, *Dramen*, Langen-Müller, München, 1968, p. 207.
3. Ibid., p. 166.
4. Ibid., p. 93.
5. Egon Vietta, *Iphigenie in Amerika*, Hamburg, 1948, p. 77.
6. Hans Henny Jahnn, *Dramen*, Vol. II, Europäische Verlagsanstalt, Frankfurt am Main, n.d. (1965), p. 617.
7. Ibid., p. 748.

4 The Theatre of Parody and the Grotesque

When black humour and 'sick jokes' were in vogue in the early sixties, it was frequently assumed that they reflected a disturbing callousness in the younger generation. To be able to laugh at suffering and death may however indicate an increase in sensitivity rather than the opposite. We live in an age when it is quite common never to have seen a corpse and yet normal to see daily reports of deaths on an unprecedented scale, in an age when conventional responses to the magnitude of the world's suffering no longer seem adequate. In our confusion laughter can provide a welcome release.

In the same way the theatre of Friedrich Dürrenmatt (b. 1921) embraces parody and the grotesque. Confronted with a world which he compares to a car being recklessly driven at breakneck speed, Dürrenmatt refuses to 'whisper amusing stories' in the ear of the driver or make the impossible attempt to get out. 'Fear, anxiety and above all anger tear open his mouth.'[1] The backward-looking drama of the *Epigonen* was not for him; on the other hand, he knew that nagging questions about the car or vociferous demands that it should stop or change direction would have little effect: not for him then the theatre that tried to come to terms with the Nazi past or the theatre that tried to achieve political change. The world has become too complex, its driving force too obscured for any of these solutions to engage Dürrenmatt. As he wrote in his *Theaterprobleme* (*Problems of the Theatre*, 1955):

> The world of today, as it appears to us, can hardly be contained in the form of Schiller's historical drama, if only because we cannot discover any tragic heroes but only tragedies which are staged by arch-butchers and carried out by mincing-machines. You cannot make a Wallenstein out of Hitler or Stalin. Their power is so immense that they themselves are only accidental, external forms of expression of this power, and the misfortune that one associates especially with the former and to some extent with the latter, is too ramified, too confused, too cruel and often all too senseless. . . . The modern state has become anonymous and bureaucratic and it is impossible to survey all its workings. . . . There are no genuine representatives and the tragic heroes have no names. . . . Art only penetrates to the victims, if it penetrates to people at all; it can no

21

longer reach the powerful. Creon's secretaries dispose of the case of Antigone.[2]

Dürrenmatt might have stopped at this point. There have been many writers whose major theme is to affirm the meaninglessness of the world and the powerlessness of their art. But significantly, there has not been a genuine Theatre of the Absurd in German-speaking countries. Admittedly there has been a strong interest in the Absurd: Karl Heinz Stroux in Düsseldorf presented the world-premieres of some of Ionesco's major plays, including *The Rhinoceroses* in 1959, and the early plays of Grass, Dorst and Michelsen were clearly influenced by Ionesco and Beckett. But one cannot claim that this was central to the development of post-war German theatre.

The reason may have been that there was no theatrical tradition in Germany. It is no good being an iconoclast unless there are a few statues around to smash. As we shall see, Handke's *Offending the Audience* would have had little impact in the bombed-out theatres of the late forties and early fifties. So when, especially in France, the Theatre of the Absurd was gaining momentum, German theatre was still floundering. By the time it had found its feet, it was striking out in quite different directions and the true inspiration of Absurdism was already past.

In addition, if one may be permitted to venture onto the treacherous ground of generalising about national attitudes, it would seem that the Germans tend to think things through to their logical extreme. While the French, English and Irish absurdists apparently accept the contradiction that they can devote their lives to asserting that life is meaningless, I suspect that a German would take his own statement more seriously: if he did not commit suicide, he would at least stop writing.

Interestingly, the only important German playwright to identify himself as an absurdist, Wolfgang Hildesheimer (b. 1916 in Hamburg), lived for several years in England and was a British information officer in Jerusalem during the last war. In his trilogy of plays *Spiele in denen es dunkel wird* (*Plays in Which Darkness Falls*) he presents visions of decline and decay. *Pastorale oder Die Zeit für Kakao* (*Pastoral or Time for Cocoa*, premiere 1958 Kammerspiele Munich) shows four cliché-ridden singers, two of whom die at the approach of winter. *Landschaft mit Figuren* (*Landscape with Figures*, premiere 1959 Tribüne West Berlin) takes place in an artist's studio in which three people are reduced to lifeless *objets d'art*, while a glazier fills the window-frames with dark violet panes. In *Die Uhren* (*The Clocks*, premiere 1959 Schlosstheater Celle) a glazier again shuts out the light with dark panes while the room of a married couple becomes filled with clocks.

In his speech on the Theatre of the Absurd at the Erlangen Festival in 1960, Hildesheimer quoted the words of Camus: 'The absurd arises from a confrontation between man who questions and the world which remains unreasonably silent.'[3] Thus the darkness that falls in each play is not only a metaphor of death but also of the opaqueness of the absurd world about us.

But Dürrenmatt rejects this total capitulation by Hildesheimer. For him the world may be grotesque, but not absurd. The difference is that the grotesque presupposes a norm while the absurd denies that any norm exists. As an example of grotesque comedy Dürrenmatt considers the possibility that Scott of the Antarctic, instead of dying in the snowy wastes, got locked in a deep-freeze a few yards from a busy street. His situation is grotesque because it is at once shocking and comic. The comedy derives from the triviality of his fate, but for it to be trivial we must have some sense of the heroism of Scott's actual death in the Antarctic. The absurdist would show the futility of all human endeavour by showing Scott 'already transformed into an ice-block sitting opposite other ice-blocks, soliloquising without any answer from his companions, without any certainty that they can hear him.'[4] While the absurdist affirms the facelessness of the world, the playwright of the grotesque attempts to give it a face, even if it is only the mask of a clown.

Equally, one might call Dürrenmatt the writer of paradox: convinced of the chaos of the world, he attempts to give it meaning; assured of the powerlessness of the individual, he praises the exercise of courage:

> . . . the universal escapes my grasp. I refuse to find the universal in a doctrine, I regard it as chaos. The world (and with it the stage which represents this world) stands before me as something monstrous, as a riddle of misfortune that must be accepted but before which there must be no capitulation.[5]

Dürrenmatt did not arrive at once at his characteristic style of grotesque comedy. His first plays were heavily written compared with his later work and owed much to Expressionism and even to Baroque drama with its themes of appearance and reality. They also contain a strong religious element, perhaps a result of Dürrenmatt's upbringing as the son of a Bernese pastor. *Es steht geschrieben* (*It Is Written*, 1946, premiere 1947 Schauspielhaus Zurich) dealt with the Anabaptists in Münster at the time of the Reformation. In 1967 Dürrenmatt rewrote it under the title *Die Wiedertäufer* (*The Anabaptists*, premiere 1967 Schauspielhaus Zurich). *Der Blinde* (*The Blind One*, 1947, premiere 1948 Stadttheater Basle) has as its central figure a serene blind duke unaware of the devastation suffered by his country in the Thirty Years' War. It was also at this time—1948—that Dürrenmatt began work on his one biblical play, *Ein Engel kommt nach Babylon* (*An Angel Comes to Babylon*), which he completed in 1953 (premiere 1953 Kammerspiele Munich) and revised in 1957. It shows events leading up to the building of the Tower of Babel and has as its hero the beggar Akki who pitches his hard-won riches into the River Euphrates.

Es steht geschrieben and *Der Blinde* were unmitigated failures. To preserve a proper sense of order, in the best Swiss manner, it is normal for the police to remove from theatres anybody who expresses his disapproval too loudly. In the case of the premiere of *Es steht geschrieben* the police could no longer cope, so great was the audience's hostility. *Der Blinde* did not fare much better, and it may have been these experiences that nudged Dürrenmatt towards his much lighter and popular style:

> Literature must become so light that it no longer tips the scales of

modern literary criticism. Only in this way will it become weighty again.[6]

Certainly he has achieved staggering success with his prescription of lightness. Since the mid-fifties Dürrenmatt has consistently been one of the five most frequently produced living playwrights, and over the last decade he heads the list with almost twice as many productions as his nearest rival, Peter Hacks. Only Shakespeare, Brecht, Molière and Schiller have been better represented.

The first play in the new style, 'A heavy, difficult comedy because apparently light and easy',[7] was *Romulus der Grosse* (*Romulus the Great*, 1948, premiere 1949 Stadttheater Basle, revised 1957 and 1961). Like Akki, Romulus, the Emperor of Rome, is an anti-hero. The Roman Empire is crumbling as the Germanic hordes invade from the north, but Romulus' main concern is with his chickens. He could save the Empire by forcing his daughter to marry the Germanic trouser-manufacturer Cäsar Rupf, but he refuses to sacrifice her in this way. Later we learn that she, her fiancé and her mother have all drowned on their flight to Sicily. Romulus' followers despise him for his supposed weakness and there is even a feeble attempt to assassinate him (a parody of the killing of Julius Caesar). The only person who understands his wisdom is the Germanic prince Odoaker, who even begs him to remain as ruler before the Germani finally become a 'bloody nation of heroes'. Romulus would prefer death, but they compromise on his going into retirement. The world is left to be taken over soon by the young Germanic thug, Theoderich.

In this play there are a number of themes that were to recur in Dürrenmatt's later plays. Above all we see the quiet courage of Romulus who faces with serenity the fall of his empire and his own personal danger. Never again was Dürrenmatt to show a man of power in such a favourable light, presumably because it contains the very idealism about enlightened rule in which Dürrenmatt could soon no longer believe. Romulus is also an agent of justice, and justice becomes a major preoccupation of the later plays. In this case Romulus' inactivity seals the deserved fate of Rome:

> I have not betrayed my empire, Rome has betrayed itself. It knew the truth but it chose force; it knew humanity but it chose tyranny. ... It is a matter of justice. ... Have we still the right to defend ourselves?[8]

Most importantly, a grotesque vision of the world is presented here: the world-ruler who turns out to be a chicken-breeder, his future son-in-law who has suffered so much in battle that his own fiancée cannot recognise him, the trouser-manufacturer whose wealth can decide the course of history. Above all we see the grotesque failure of good intentions: Romulus saves his daughter from an unhappy marriage only for her to drown the next day, and Odoaker and Romulus confer about the maintenance of peace in the full knowledge that Theoderich will soon create an empire bloodier than that of Rome. It is tempting to assume that these acts, because fruitless, are also meaningless. But this is to judge by results, to base moral judgments on a profit and loss account. For Dürrenmatt the unheroic act of giving 'sense to nonsense' is meaningful in itself.

These considerations also apply to Count Übelohe in Dürrenmatt's next play, *Die Ehe des Herrn Mississippi* (*The Marriage of Mr. Mississippi*, 1950, premiere 1952 Kammerspiele Munich, revised 1957 and 1970). Übelohe flees to Africa under the false impression that he is accomplice to a murder, opens a hospital there and ruins his health; but native medicine proves stronger and the whole enterprise is a failure: 'it always took a turn for the ridiculous'. Again, the inherent value of the action weighs more than anything that can be achieved in this 'riddle of misfortune' called the world. *Mississippi*, which was the first of Dürrenmatt's big premieres, directed as it was by Hans Schweikart, is the most ostensibly political of his plays. This is one reason why he has twice felt the need to update the play, for, as he once observed: 'A play is never completed. It becomes.'[10] In an involved plot of rebellion, counter-rebellion and multiple poisonings the five main characters have little more substance than the views they represent: Anastasia lives for the moment and has no moral scruples; Mississippi, the Public Prosecutor, is the representative of harsh Old Testament justice; Saint-Claude, the Communist, is the champion of social justice; Diego is the pragmatist who will adapt to any political situation; and Übelohe, physically the most decadent yet the only positive figure of the piece, seeks to transform the world through the power of love.

More interesting than the rather convoluted action is the playful use of the stage. Written at a time when Ionesco's *The Bald Prima-Donna* had only just been premiered and Beckett's plays were yet to be seen, *Mississippi* displays many adventurous techniques later to be identified as absurdist. The grotesque exaggerations, the sudden entrances and exits (in one case from and into a grandfather clock), the surrealistic setting with one window giving onto a northern scene and another revealing a southern landscape: such devices were to become the stock-in-trade of the Theatre of the Absurd. It is undoubtedly true that Dürrenmatt himself owed much to Thornton Wilder, whose *Our Town* in 1939 and *The Skin of Our Teeth* in 1944 caused great interest in their Zurich performances, but the boldness and originality of Dürrenmatt's dramatic method is still generally underestimated.

The play with which he achieved international fame and possibly still the best known post-war German drama is *Der Besuch der alten Dame* (*The Visit*, 1955, premiere 1956 Schauspielhaus Zurich). This 'tragic comedy' is again concerned with justice, here wielded in a monstrous way by the power of capital. Claire Zachanassian, an ageing multi-millionairess, has returned to the village of her birth, the decaying and cheerless Güllen (the name in Swiss German means 'liquid-manure'). She is a grotesque, unreal figure: almost all her limbs are artificial, and she is surrounded by a retinue of grotesques, including the most recent of her many husbands. The purpose of 'the visit' is to wreak vengeance on one of the community, Alfred Ill, who in his youth had bribed witnesses in a paternity case so that he might disown Claire and abandon her and her child in favour of another wealthier village girl. Claire is now prepared to offer a vast amount of money to restore the village to prosperity, if the community agrees to dispose of Ill. The mayor rejects her proposal in horror, but the community is gradually seduced by the promise of riches: 'at first determined to reject the offer, they incur debts, not with the intention of killing Ill, but carelessly, from a feeling

25

that everything will sort itself out.'[11] When Ill sees everyone wearing yellow shoes, the symbol of the new prosperity—even his own family has bought a car—he recognises that his fate is inevitable. After a half-hearted attempt to escape, he resigns himself to his death and is killed ceremonially at a public meeting.

Der Besuch der alten Dame shows, like Max Frisch's *Andorra*, a community persecuting one of their number, for here Claire Zachanassian is merely the trigger of the conflict which takes place between the villagers and Ill. But whereas in *Andorra* Frisch examines the workings of racial prejudice and offers his model as a corrective, Dürrenmatt presents the power of capital and the corruptibility of society as an unalterable fact. Human freedom is not to be exercised in the futile attempt to change the immutable but in attaining to the quiet courage and serenity achieved by Ill before his death. In his belief that man ultimately asserts his freedom in the acceptance of his own death, Dürrenmatt shows himself to stand astonishingly close to Schiller.

If the power of capital is the moving force behind *Der Besuch der alten Dame*, in *Die Physiker* it is the power of nuclear physics. *Die Physiker* (*The Physicists*, 1961, premiere 1962 Schauspielhaus Zurich), which has been directed by Peter Brook, is Dürrenmatt's other great international success. This time the plot begins with a murder: one of the nurses in an exclusive psychiatric clinic has been strangled by a patient who believes himself to be Einstein. In the same section of the clinic are two further physicists, 'Newton' and Möbius, who imagines himself in the power of King Solomon. The First Act ends with Möbius murdering another nurse who has fallen in love with him and arranged his release. After the interval the confusions of the first half are explained. Möbius is a brilliant nuclear physicist who has pretended to be mad in order to withhold his dangerous secrets from a world that would certainly use them to destroy itself. He was forced to kill the nurse whose faith in him threatened the future of the human race. Moreover, it turns out that 'Newton' and 'Einstein' are not mad either: they are agents, the one American, the other Russian, who have dissembled insanity in order to get close to Möbius' secret discoveries. Failing to convince Möbius that he should release his findings, they are easily and implausibly persuaded to join him in his vow of silence and all three resolve to end their days in the asylum. So far, so good: we have the characteristic unheroic heroism of withdrawal, the courage of those who are prepared to remain in a madhouse to prevent the world becoming one: 'Crazy but wise. Captive but free. Physicists but innocent.'[12] But the play is not over yet, for 'A story is thought through to its conclusion when it has taken its worst possible twist.'[13] It transpires that the woman doctor in charge of the clinic has stolen all Möbius' discoveries and has begun to found a world-empire with them. It is she who really believes herself in the power of King Solomon. Despite all Möbius' efforts, the future of the world is in the hands of a madwoman, for 'What has once been thought can no longer be taken back.'[14]

In this tightly constructed play Dürrenmatt again shows himself to be intensely pessimistic without being nihilistic. The world is buried in dung and there is no hope of its being cleared; at most the individual can transform a small part of it into a fertile garden. This is the image underlying Dürrenmatt's parodistic treatment of Hercules' fifth labour in

Herkules und der Stall des Augias (*Hercules and the Augean Stable*, radio-play 1954, stage-play 1962, premiere 1963 Schauspielhaus Zurich). When the old-time hero has failed to cleanse the 'stable' because of bureaucratic interference and leaves Elis under its mountain of dung, Augias takes his son into the garden he has cultivated. With the subtlety of a sledge hammer Augias gives a statement of the author's philosophy:

> I am a politician, my son, and not a hero, and politics cannot work miracles. . . . So I did what is good. I transformed dung into soil. It is a difficult time when we are able to do so little for the world, but we ought at least to do what we can. . . . Dare to live now and to live here in the middle of this formless barren land, not contented but discontented, passing on your discontent and so changing things with time.[15]

This is a quiet bourgeois withdrawal from the 'riddle of misfortune', a withdrawal that Frisch depicts so negatively in *Biedermann und die Brandstifter*. It stands in the tradition of those who retire from posing the grand questions to a personally meaningful existence, the tradition of the Austrian Adalbert Stifter with his praise of 'effectiveness in one's own sphere' or of Voltaire in *Candide* with the famous dictum: 'il faut cultiver le jardin'.

It is therefore predictable that Dürrenmatt should turn towards more private, domestic drama. Not that he has abandoned social and political themes, as witnessed by his adaptations of Shakespeare, *König Johann* (*King John*, premiere 1968 Basler Theater) and *Titus Andronicus* (premiere 1970 Schauspielhaus Düsseldorf), and by his apocalyptic vision in *Porträt eines Planeten* (*Portrait of a Planet*, premiere 1970 Schauspielhaus Düsseldorf). Similarly, his most recent play, *Der Mitmacher* (*The Conniver*, 1972, premiere 1973 Schauspielhaus Zurich) recalls his earlier grotesque visions of a world controlled by malevolent forces. The mass-murderer who disposes of his corpses by dissolving them in a 'necrodialysator' is replaced by the state which will continue to put the machine to their own uses. But his two most significant pieces since *Die Physiker* have dealt with more personal situations.

In *Der Meteor* (*The Meteor*, premiere 1966 Schauspielhaus Zurich) the playfulness that was evident in *Die Ehe des Herrn Mississippi* reaches its full maturity; of his black comedies it is the least dark, even though it deals with death. The protagonist is a man who dies twice and who at the end of the play is still waiting for his third and final death: Wolfgang Schwitter, Nobel Prize winner for literature, appears suddenly in the studio in which he had once lived as an impoverished painter before becoming a successful writer. He has just died in the clinic (or so he is told later) but he wishes to die alone in his old bed, in his old room. After various interruptions he dies again in the act of making love to one of the present occupants of the room, the wife of the painter Nyffenschwander. He is duly laid in state again, only to revive soon afterwards. The doctor establishes that he is healthier than ever before, while almost everyone who comes into contact with him dies: the parson who comes to comfort him, his young wife who commits suicide after he has rejected her, Nyffenschwander who is thrown down the stairs by Muheim, the landlord, himself later arrested for murder. One of the last visitors is his mother-in-law, an old toilet-attendant, who mourns the fact that her daughter, a successful call-girl, had given up her promising profession to marry Schwitter, for with prostitutes as with writers 'You shouldn't have feelings, you should make them.'[16] Then she too expires. The play closes with the Salvation Army bursting in and Schwitter calling out for his 'final' death.

According to Dürrenmatt, '*Der Meteor* is a play about being unable to believe.'[17] Schwitter cannot believe in his own resurrection from the dead. As a sceptic he represents modern Christianity's inability to have faith in itself. More generally, because he regards death as the one absolute certainty about existence, this throws his life into doubt: 'Schwitter does not achieve eternal life but eternal dying.'[18] It is the simple faith of the Salvation Army, bubbling over with noise and life that is set against the nihilism of Schwitter:

> Life is an incomparably evil trick played by Nature, an obscene aberration of carbon, a malevolent festering of the earth's surface, an incurable scab.[19]

This is also the most biographical of Dürrenmatt's plays, expressing fashionable doubts about his function as a writer. There is a strong element of self-questioning in the critic's speech at Schwitter's death-bed:

> It was his nihilism that made him a moralist. . . . His work was the expression of impotence, not an image of reality: his theatre, not reality, is grotesque.[20]

Setting philosophical interpretation and biographical allusions aside, *Der Meteor* is a highly amusing comedy of the macabre. Typically for Dürrenmatt, the insubstantiality of the characters and the austerely constructed plot with its witty and implausible peripeteiae are more reminiscent of the revue sketch than of serious drama. He may, as he had hoped, have won over his audiences by the use of comedy, but one may fairly ask what he has won them over to.

The merits and demerits of his dramatic style can be well observed in his adaptation of Strindberg's *Dance of Death*, *Play Strindberg* (1968–69, premiere 1969 Basler Theater). This play has enjoyed colossal success: it was given fifty different productions in its first two seasons alone, establishing it at once as the most frequently staged contemporary play of the last decade. It is ideally suited to studio performance, having a cast of three and a single set. Moreover, this 'play for actors'[21] offers the public the dual attraction of a 'classic' and a new work by a living author.

Dürrenmatt presents Strindberg's play as the twelve rounds of a boxing-match between Alice and Edgar, with Kurt initially acting as a kind of referee but then revealing himself very much as a participant. The alterations to the original are primarily in the interest of economy: the language is stripped to a bare minimum, the verbal exchanges are no longer Strindberg's slow turning of a knife in the wound but the sharp blows of a prize-fighter. There are also attempts to clarify and polarise: when Edgar threatens to re-marry, he here names Kurt's ex-wife as his bride, and there are several references to a former relationship between Alice and Kurt (this and the 'photo-album scene' apparently owe more to Ibsen's *Hedda Gabler* than to *Dance of Death*). When the accusation of embezzlement here becomes an invention by Alice, we see that Dürrenmatt is steering the story onto his own well-worn tracks. From the 'Seventh Round' onwards the action becomes more grotesque: Edgar is reduced to babbling infantility and Kurt reveals himself as a master-criminal. Kurt's visit has reinforced his immorality, for 'In the world outside in which I live things are no worse. Only the dimensions are different.'[22] The mutual exploitation and savagery of Edgar and Alice's marriage is a microcosm of the world as Dürrenmatt sees it.

Dürrenmatt decided to revise Strindberg because he was disturbed by what he called the 'plush x infinity' of the original. Yet it is this very plush, the realism of the bourgeois setting, that lends *Dance of Death* much of its power: the horror creeps out of the tower-walls in a mysterious and indefinable manner. By abstracting and clarifying, Dürrenmatt has robbed the original of most of its impact. The plush drawing-room has given way to the sterile operating-theatre.

In *Die Ehe des Herrn Mississippi* the curtain closes for the interval, the house-lights go up and the audience prepare to leave their seats. At this point Übelohe makes his first entrance and begs leave to be heard. Not only is this a striking *coup de théâtre*; more importantly, it utilises the wave of annoyance that an audience must feel when the proper order of events is disturbed and they are delayed from their interval drinks. At once Übelohe is established as a nuisance: theatre convention is pressed into service to condition our attitude to one of the characters.

Fourteen years later this kind of device was used as the basis of an hour-long play—Peter Handke's *Publikumsbeschimpfung* (*Offending the Audience*, 1965, premiere 1966 Theater am Turm Frankfurt, directed by Claus Peymann). Handke (b. 1942 in Carinthia, Austria) is without question the most controversial of modern German playwrights, variously regarded as a charlatan or a genius, or possibly a genius at charlatanism. What is anyway clear is that in a theatre hardly distinguished by its experimentation, Handke's has been the most original mind for decades. Like Dürrenmatt, he does not believe his writing can materially affect reality. For him literature cannot directly reflect reality because its necessary concern with style leads to inevitable distortions: 'Even so-called committed literature, although it calls itself realistic, is unrealistic and romantic.'[23] In an essay significantly entitled *Ich bin ein Bewohner des Elfenbeinturms* (*I am an Ivory-Tower Dweller*, 1967) Handke states that he has only one theme:

> To become clear, clearer about myself, to get to know myself or not, to learn what I do wrong, what I think wrong, what I think thoughtlessly, what I say thoughtlessly, what I say automatically, what others too thoughtlessly do, think and say . . . to make others and to become myself more sensitive, more precise, so that I and others too can exist more precisely and more sensitively, so that I can communicate better with others and relate better to them.[24]

Living in the ivory-tower does not therefore mean the aesthete's disregard for reality. Again like Dürrenmatt, Handke sees the most valuable function of his work in affecting the individual, who in turn may help to change society. It is guerrilla warfare rather than frontal attack.

In *Publikumsbeschimpfung*, which was the success of the week at the first 'Experimenta' in Frankfurt in 1966, Handke presented a significant challenge to the 'thoughtless thinking' of the public. The audience is ushered into the theatre with even more solemnity than usual and those whose clothing is too informal are refused admittance. When the curtain rises, the stage is empty but for four 'speakers' (not 'actors') who, after initially ignoring the audience, begin to address them. At first, the speakers destroy any illusions the audience might have about the nature of the piece. They then make statements about the relationship of the audience to the stage: they even congratulate the spectators on being so life-like, such good performers. In the final section they intersperse insults among the compliments, rising to a crescendo of abuse. As Nicholas Hern has pointed out in his excellent study of Handke, the play, especially the preamble in the theatre, is in the nature of a practical joke that does not bear repetition.[25] But Handke claims for it only that it is a 'prologue', in particular 'the prologue to your future theatre-visits.'[26] What he has attempted to do is to demystify the ritual of theatre-going, to make others 'more sensitive and more precise' about the conventions of the theatre. It is not an anti-play but 'a playgoer's play, and far from being anti, it depends on the theatre as an institution' (Hern).[27]

Since Beckett's *Waiting for Godot*, the play in which 'nothing happens—twice', no written piece had stripped the theatre so bare: there is no plot, no characterisation, no relationships (except that established spontaneously between speakers and audience) and very little development. Handke had risen to sudden fame with this play, but where could he go from here? For a while, less successful *Sprechstücke* ('speaking-pieces') continued to be performed: *Weissagung* and *Selbstbezichtigung* (*Prophecy* 1964, and *Self-Accusation*, 1965, premiere 1966 Städtische Bühnen Oberhausen) and *Hilferufe* (*Cries for Help*, premiere 1967 in Stockholm by Städtische Bühnen Oberhausen).

Then in 1968 appeared Handke's first full-length play, which Brook directed in Paris and which many rate alongside Weiss' *Marat/Sade* as the most important product of post-war German theatre—*Kaspar* (premiere 1968 Theater am Turm Frankfurt, directed by Peymann, and Städtische Bühnen Oberhausen). Here for the first time Handke employs mime, defined by extremely detailed stage-directions reminiscent of Beckett. After plays which consisted almost entirely of words, Handke now writes a piece in which the protagonist must first learn to speak. His name derives from the historical figure of Kaspar Hauser who allegedly spent the first 16 years of his life imprisoned in a chicken coop. When in 1828 he was found wandering the streets of Nuremberg in an understandably confused state, he could speak only one sentence: 'I want to become a horseman like my father was once.' In Handke's play this is refined to: 'I want to become someone like somebody else was once.' Kaspar, an innocent clown-like figure, stumbles around on the stage, trying to come to terms with his own environment. He repeats his one sentence while three voices bombard him with speech. Gradually these voices destroy Kaspar's sentence and he begins the slow process of learning language. With more linguistic control he gains more confidence; for now that he can name things, he can establish order. This confidence grows as he is joined by other identical Kaspars, until he pronounces all the rules of social propriety. But this is followed by disintegration, as he declares, 'Every sentence / is for the birds',[28] and asserts that language is inadequate as a means of expression. Finally his words no longer make any sense and as the curtain jerks shut, he utters his last sentence: 'I am I only by chance.'[29]

This play, which Handke himself describes as 'Sprechfolterung' ('speech-torture'), shows his preoccupation with language as something which can destroy innocence, distort perception and be used as an instrument of oppression, Just as *Publikumsbeschimpfung* makes the audience attentive to the clichés of the theatre, so *Kaspar* makes them aware of the clichés of language itself.

Predictably, Handke's next play contained no spoken words at all. *Der Mündel will Vormund sein* (*My Foot, My Tutor*, premiere 1969 Theater am Turm Frankfurt, directed by Peymann) presents a series of scenes in which a guardian establishes his dominance over his ward. It contains a number of startling and ambiguous visual images, for example the shortest scene of the piece:

> Suddenly we see that the ward's nose is bleeding. The blood runs from his nose, over his mouth, over his chin, from his nose . . .
> The guardian sits motionless, the ward does not move from his place nor on his place . . .
> Gradually it becomes slowly dark on the stage again . . .[30]

Much of the ward's behaviour in his silent, melancholy ineptitude recalls Buster Keaton, and the silent-film idiom is explored again in *Der Ritt über den Bodensee* (*The Ride Across Lake Constance*, premiere 1970 Schaubühne am Halleschen Ufer, directed by Peymann and Wolfgang Wiens). This was Handke's next play, apart from the ingenious but unsatisfactory experiment in ambiguity, *Quodlibet* (premiere 1970 Basler Theater). Once again, for the third time in four years, Handke had pulled it off: a play that flew in the face of all dramatic conventions and yet was by no means a repetition of his previous work. The five main participants, who are all named after famous actors and actresses of the silent-film era, perform gestures, adopt poses and utter sentences with dream-like incoherence. The title is derived from a ballad by Gustav Schwab (1792–1850), which tells of a horseman who, without knowing it, rides across the frozen Lake Constance. When he looks back and sees the ice breaking, he suddenly recognises the risk he has run and dies of fright. He dies therefore not from any real cause, but as a result of his mental processes. This is what is reflected in Handke's play—people in a dream, people in a film, living at one remove from reality, isolated from one another, constantly misinterpreting each other's signals. One example must suffice: Emil Jannings has dropped his cigar-box. In the course of conversation he gestures with an open palm. His interlocutor, Heinrich George, looks at Jannings' hand, imagining the gesture to be a demand that he should pick up the cigar-box. Because George appears interested in his hand, Jannings hold his pose. George finally reaches for the cigar-box and hands it to Jannings, who protests that his gesture was not meant in this way. Such trivial incidents and theatrical gags (someone falling when somebody else has been kicked), together with the dream-like moves and phrases, are the material from which Handke has constructed his second full-length play. Having challenged the audience's attitudes to theatre and to language, he now questions thought-processes: are we interpreting reality 'sensitively and precisely', or are we, like the horseman, destroying ourselves by concern about what we think might have been reality?

It is no small achievement to have created a play on such an 'interior' subject, and with each new surprise the critics wonder in which direction Handke will next move. His latest play has taken a step back towards more conventional dramaturgy. *Die Unvernünftigen sterben aus* (*They Are Dying Out*, premiere 1974 Theater am Neumarkt Zurich) has almost the rudiments of a plot: the manager of a large firm goes back on an agreement made with his shareholders. He strangles a particularly annoying shareholder and then kills himself by ramming his head several times against a rock. To judge by the title, this is intended as some sort of optimistic vision of the self-defeat of capitalism, but while the style of the play may be more orthodox, the meaning remains obscure.

Whatever one may feel about Handke, he cannot be ignored. From the age of 24 he has repeatedly found new ways of confronting the theatre and its public and has, remarkably, remained extremely popular in the process. In the last ten years he has been the third most frequently produced contemporary German-language playwright, a considerable achievement for a young *avant-garde* author (although it is questionable whether he is as *avant-garde* as he claims, if the old guard of the German theatre are marching along beside him). There is a danger with such clever and articulate young writers that the audience is impaled on a fork: if Handke's work is admired, his talent is recognised; if not, then this is sure proof that he is a misunderstood genius like Ibsen, Brecht and Beckett before him.

Dispensing with language or using it with the purpose of undermining its own meaning necessarily leads to ambiguities. And ambiguities lead to the situation where all interpretations are valid. And where all interpretations are valid, none are. I find it for example disturbing that the final sentence of *Kaspar*: 'I am I only by chance', is rendered in the English translation as 'Goats and monkeys, Goats and monkeys.'[31] If the final sentence is anyway meaningless and therefore replaceable by a phrase taken from the preceding speech, I cannot conceive why it was written.

Handke's great talent lies in his ingenuity. He has hit upon some truly startling ideas and created new frames of reference. *Der Ritt über den Bodensee* makes one more aware of the somnambulistic rituals which form so much of daily living, just as Pinter will attune one's ears to the incoherences of everyday conversation. Unfortunately, when Handke exhausts one of his brilliant ideas, he tends to exhaust the audience in the process.

Notes to Chapter 4

1. *Theaterprobleme*, Arche, Zurich, new edn., 1963, p. 57f.
2. Ibid., p. 43f.

3. 'Über das absurde Theater', *Deutsche Dramaturgie der Sechziger Jahre*, ed. Gotthart Wunberg, Max Niemeyer, Tübingen, 1974, p. 6.
4. *Komödien*, Vol. III, Arche, Zurich, 1966, p. 175.
5. *Theaterprobleme*, p. 49.
6. Ibid., p. 60.
7. *Komödien*, Vol. I, Arche, Zurich, 1957, p. 85.
8. Ibid., p. 65f.
9. Ibid., p. 137.
10. From programme notes to his own production of *Der Besuch der alten Dame*, Ateliertheater Berne, 1959.
11. *Komödien* I, p. 352.
12. *Komödien*, Vol. II, Arche, Zurich, 1959, p. 344.
13. Ibid., p. 353.
14. Ibid., p. 350.
15. Ibid., p. 428.
16. *Komödien* III, p. 71.
17. *Dramaturgisches und Kritisches*, Arche, Zurich, 1972, p. 159.
18. Ibid., p. 160.
19. *Komödien*, III, p. 74.
20. Ibid., p. 45.
21. Ibid., p. 349.
22. Ibid., p. 347.
23. 'Die Literatur ist romantisch', *Prosa Gedichte Theaterstücke Hörspiel Aufsätze*, Suhrkamp, Frankfurt, 1969, p. 286.
24. Ibid., p. 270.
25. *Peter Handke*, Wolff, London, 1971, p. 33f.
26. *Publikumsbeschimpfung und andere Sprechstücke*, Suhrkamp, Frankfurt, 1966, p. 42.
27. *Peter Handke*, p. 37.
28. *Kaspar*, Suhrkamp, Frankfurt, 1968, p. 92.
29. Ibid., p. 101f.
30. *Prosa Gedichte* etc., p. 174.
31. *Kaspar*, transl. by Michael Roloff, Methuen, London, 1972, p. 98f.

5 The Theatre That Came to Terms With the Past

While many post-war playwrights averted their gaze from the horrors of the present to look backwards to the theatre of history and myth, and yet others squinted mockingly at the world about them, there were also a substantial number who looked the recent German past squarely in the eye. This widespread attempt to understand the roots of Fascism and to expiate the guilt of the German nation earned the label 'Bewältigung der Vergangenheit' ('coming to terms with the past'). Initially plays were written about the war itself; in the fifties there followed allegorical dramas about the Nazi past; and in the sixties a number of dramas examined modern West German society in its relationship to Fascism. Born of the same concerns, but using different dramatic means, were the first documentary dramas of the sixties, which will be considered in Chapter 8. Indeed, Peter Weiss' *Die Ermittlung* (*The Investigation*, 1965) might be regarded as the final exorcism of the eventually somewhat obsessive 'Bewältigung der Vergangenheit'.

Curiously, the first play that tried to come to terms with the past, written and produced even before the war was over, was the work not of a German, but of a Swiss: Max Frisch's *Nun singen sie wieder* (*Now They've Started Singing Again*, 1945, premiere March 1945 Schauspielhaus Zurich). Indeed, Frisch felt that the neutrality of his country placed upon him a special responsibility. As he wrote in his *Tagebuch* (*Diary*) *1946–49:*

> We did not experience the war in our own sufferings . . . [but] our good fortune was only apparent. We lived on the edge of a torture-chamber, we heard the cries, but it was not ourselves that cried. . . . We may wish for things passionately but we do not share the compulsion of the fighter, we do not share his temptation to take revenge. Perhaps that is the real gift that has been granted to those who have been spared, and also their real task. Perhaps they possess the now rare freedom to judge fairly. What is more, they are obliged to. It is the only means of retaining dignity in the midst of suffering nations.[1]

Thus Max Frisch (b. 1911) shares the same paradox as his compatriot Dürrenmatt in that—for all his international concern and world-wide fame—his writing is firmly rooted in his national identity as

34

a Swiss. Though ten years older than Dürrenmatt, Frisch began writing plays at about the same time (with *Santa Cruz* in 1944), having worked as both journalist and architect, a profession he did not finally abandon until 1955.

Nun singen sie wieder in its determination to 'judge fairly' is not concerned with apportioning blame or examining causes. It is, as the subtitle states, an 'Attempt at a Requiem', an expression of sorrow at the sufferings of Europe and a plea for reconciliation. In a series of unrealistic scenes we are confronted with the horrors of war: the shooting of defenceless hostages, an air-raid on defenceless civilians, the suicide of a deserter and the execution of a school-teacher whose cowardice made him condone the Nazi barbarism but who finally speaks out against it. In the second half of the play the dead are brought together in a ruined abbey where the hostages had sung as they were being executed. 'Now they've started singing again', as they sit celebrating a form of communion. The necessary act of reconciliation is to be achieved through self-examination in this after-life. As the abbey priest says:

> I believe we are all here to get to know the life that we could have led together. Until then we must remain here. That is our remorse, our damnation and our redemption.[2]

The solutions to the horror perpetrated by man on his fellow-man seem to lie in a vague humanist pacifism, with neo-Rousseauist implications of the value of simple living: the idyllic elements of the after-life apparently consist of baking bread and fetching wine, and both the 'German' deserter's wife and the 'British' Air Force Captain dream of returning to Nature, she of living in the woods with her husband, he of keeping sheep like his grandfather.

It would no doubt be unfair to demand any deeper analysis than that offered by this 'Requiem', written when the devastation of war was still so immediate. Nevertheless, this play established three themes that were to remain central to Frisch's writing. First, there was the question of guilt, how it was that otherwise normal and loving people could turn so easily to violence and brutality. Secondly, there was Frisch's search for an answer to this in the recognition that we create for ourselves a fixed image of others, thereby reducing them to objects whose sufferings leave us unmoved (so in *Nun singen sie wieder* each side repeatedly says of the other: 'They're devils! They're devils!'). Thirdly, Frisch expressed here his scepticism about the power of art to change anything. All the love of the school-teacher for things of beauty does not save him from compromising himself with the Nazis, and the splendour of Bach's *Matthew Passion* seems an illusion beside the harsh realities of war. Finally, as the survivors bring wreaths to the graves of their fallen comrades, promising to avenge their deaths, they are unable to hear the dead calling upon them to seek reconciliation instead. The dead have died in vain, and in their inability to pass on their lessons to the living, Frisch is expressing his doubts about the efficacy of his own writing. The ending, if unanalytical, is at least not sentimental.

A similarly stylised portrayal of war was provided by Wolfgang Borchert's *Draussen vor der Tür* (*The Man Outside*, 1947, premiere 1947 Kammerspiele Hamburg). Although, with inverted arrogance, he sub-titled it 'A play that no theatre wishes to perform and no public wishes to see', it has enjoyed considerable success on the post-war German stage. The radio-broadcast of the play in February 1947 already brought Borchert such immediate fame that he eventually complained to reporters and the public: 'I'm not a specimen on display!' *Draussen vor der Tür* has been made into a film, translated into several languages, and to this day hardly a year passes without at least two German theatres performing it. Since it is not a well-written piece, the reasons for its popularity must be sought elsewhere. The close association between the drama and the fate of its author has helped. He died at the age of 26, mainly as a result of his war-wounds, one day before the stage-premiere in Hamburg. He had been twice imprisoned by the Nazis, not for any decisive political utterances, which might have made him suspect to post-war audiences, but for general criticism of the conduct of the war. A victim of the war and of Fascist tyranny, his youthful death was almost bound to win the sympathy of the public.

It is the same sympathy which operates in favour of the central figure of Borchert's play, Beckmann. We see this soldier returned from the wars, wandering from scene to scene, only to discover that he is alone and unwanted, 'the man outside'. His parents are dead, his wife has left him, his Colonel cannot understand him and the director of a cabaret cannot employ him as a singer because he states the truth too directly. With this, the audience is blackmailed, were it still necessary, into feeling sorry for Beckmann and listening to his self-pitying story. The single emotion of the play is pathos: even God is 'tearful' because no-one believes in him any more. Despair itself would have more energy than this.

Not only is the audience comfortingly allowed to pity itself in pitying Beckmann; it is also reassured by a dramatic style that has the semblance of modernity without any of the attendant complications. The personification of figures like God, Death (as a roadsweeper!) and the River Elbe are derived from mediaeval drama by way of Expressionism, and the language betrays similar Expressionistic elements. In *Das ist unser Manifest* (*That Is Our Manifesto*, c. 1939) Borchert had stated:

> We don't need poets with good grammar. We have not enough patience for grammar. We need poets who sob their feelings hot and hoarse. Who call a tree a tree and a woman a woman and say yes and say no. Loud and clear and three times over and without conjunctions.[3]

It all sounds like someone who has belatedly jumped aboard the Expressionist train without noticing that it has come to a halt. Written in eight days, *Draussen vor der Tür* suffers from a mannered and repetitive style which abounds in abstract concepts, thus giving the audience the impression that it is hearing philosophy without being troubled by thinking.

Astonishingly, the first play to treat war in a realistic manner was again written by a playwright living outside Germany, the exiled Carl Zuckmayer. Born in 1896, he fought as an officer in the First World War, worked as a *Dramaturg* together with Brecht at the Deutsches Theater Berlin and then made his reputation as a playwright in the nineteen-twenties and thirties with such plays as *Der Hauptmann von Köpenick* (*The Captain of Köpenick*, 1931). He later came into conflict with the Nazis and emigrated to the United States by way of Austria and Switzerland. Assuming US nationality, he returned to Europe in 1946 in the service of his government, but finally settled in Switzerland, where he now lives in Saas-Fee. It was during his period as a farmer in Vermont that he wrote *Des Teufels General* (*The Devil's General*, 1942–45, premiere 1946 Schauspielhaus Zurich, directed by Heinz Hilpert). This play has also enjoyed considerable success on the post-war German stage. Reporting on the West German premiere of the play in Frankfurt (1947), Zuckmayer spoke of an 'emotional shock such as is seldom engendered by a stage-play. People recognised themselves in the mirror of their times.'[4] Subsequently it has been frequently revived, notably in the mid-sixties for Zuckmayer's seventieth birthday, when it was staged by twelve different theatres in two seasons (1966/67 and 1967/68), including the Schiller-Theater Berlin under the direction of Boleslaw Barlog.

The Devil's General is General Harras, an officer of the old school, who serves the 'devil' Hitler from his sheer love of flying:

> Nowhere in the world would I have been given these opportunities—these unlimited means—this power. The five years in which we set the air force on its feet were years well spent. And when an old wolf has tasted blood again, he runs with the pack and doesn't give a damn—whether you like the people in charge or not.[5]

He maintains a suicidal disregard for the Gestapo and exploits his position to help those opposed to the Nazis, even smuggling Jews out of the country. When a number of planes crash because of sabotage, he is arrested by the Gestapo and granted a ten day stay of execution to give him the opportunity to find the culprits. He finally discovers that his trusted assistant Oderbruch is responsible for sabotaging the aircraft, promises not to betray him but rejects the possibility of escaping abroad to continue the resistance to Hitler:

> Too late, my friend. I'm no longer good enough for that. If you've become the Devil's General on earth and have bombed a path for him—then you have to prepare quarters for him in hell.[6]

So he climbs aboard a defective aeroplane and kills himself.

Once again, the sources of Fascism are hardly analysed. Repeatedly, Hitler is associated with the devil, and the five beams of a searchlight appear as the five fingers of his hand holding Germany in its grasp. This equation of Fascism with the diabolical became well established in West German writing and is still recognisable in Hochhuth's figure of the Doctor in *Der Stellvertreter* (*The Representative*, 1959–62). It was in many ways a comforting belief to ascribe the insanity that overtook the German nation to diabolical forces, because it denied the need for radical social change as a means of preventing its recurrence. The political dramatists of the sixties were to argue differently.

Zuckmayer also asserts that the 'Faustian' German national character was to blame for Nazi excesses, thus creating the very sort of fixed image that Frisch was at pains to dismantle. Turning from causes to solutions, Harras' response to the Nazi regime is a kind of inner opposition based on a vague code of ethics: 'Wherever a man renews himself the world is created anew.'[7] The only active stand in the play is made by the saboteur Oderbruch, and his reasons are self-confessedly negative: the only hope for Germany is 'defeat. We thirst for ruin. We must lend a hand to bring it closer. Only then can we rise up purified.'[8] This welcoming of defeat as a means of national renewal must have been just the kind of reassurance that was needed by the war-weary German public. So they were able to overlook the stylistic faults of the play: the forced imagery, the unprepared entrances and the unrounded characters. Thirty years later it is difficult to do so.

Apart from the topical subject matter, everything else places *Des Teufels General* amongst the historical pieces discussed in Chapter 3, and Zuckmayer indeed alternated historical dramas with works on the recent past. In 1949 there was the premiere at the Deutsches Theater Constance of *Barbara Blomberg*, set in sixteenth century Spain and the Netherlands; and in 1953 the Deutsches Theater Göttingen presented the premiere of *Ulla Winblad* about the mistress of the eighteenth century Swedish poet Carl Michael Bellman.

Both of these were again directed by Heinz Hilpert, as was Zuckmayer's other war-play, *Der Gesang im Feuerofen* (*Song of the Furnace*, 1948–50, premiere 1950 Deutsches Theater Göttingen). It was based on a newspaper report about the burning to death of some twenty young members of the French Resistance who had gathered in a ruined chateau to celebrate Christmas Eve, 1943. While the French court of 1948 condemned to death the French traitor who had betrayed his fellows to the Germans, Zuckmayer is unable to judge so harshly. We are meant to regard both sides, French and Germans, as being composed of good and evil elements. The French police and the German soldiers share the same names and are to be played by the same actors. In this attempt at understanding and reconciliation, Zuckmayer establishes the notion of the interchangeability of roles, which too was to be seen in Hochhuth's *Der Stellvertreter*.

All participants of the war are shown once again to be the victims of cosmic forces: 'It is the time when Lucifer comes to the earth and nobody knows any more the difference between good and evil.'[9] Thus, in one of the mystical scenes that are interspersed among the realistic scenes of action, two angels assure the 'traitor' Louis Creveaux that all men share in his guilt. Once again Zuckmayer offers his audience a message of comfort, for where all are guilty, no-one is.

Max Frisch in his later development sought to dispense strong medicine in place of Zuckmayer's placebos. A decisive influence on Frisch was his acquaintanceship with Brecht from 1947 onwards. He spoke of the unnerving power of Brecht's dialectics: 'I am constantly beaten but not convinced.'[10] Unlike Brecht, Frisch did not believe that the theatre could change the world but only our relationship to it. The enjoyment of theatre did not require any justification on the grounds that it taught us something; and yet Frisch recognised that the theatre repeatedly showed situations in need of change.

So Frisch, like many Western writers, finds himself caught between the mythical and historical view of man. Hochwälder, Dürrenmatt, Zuckmayer and others view the world as myth, as a basically unchanging continuum with which the individuals must come to terms. Brecht and his followers see man and the world as capable of change, as part of a historical process. Frisch stands in the middle, convinced of the need to influence the world, equally convinced of his inability to do so.

In *Nun singen sie wieder* he had already expressed his doubts about the relevance of art to war, and in his next play, *Die chinesische Mauer* (*The Great Wall of China*, 1946, premiere 1946 Schauspielhaus Zurich, directed by Leonard Steckel), he shows the powerlessness of the poet in the atomic age. When the poet, 'the Man of Today', denounces the Emperor for his injustice, the Emperor responds by awarding him the annual prize for the best apocalyptic vision.

Significantly, the Man of Today is a Doctor of Jurisprudence. So he adumbrates the Doctor of Philosophy who proclaims revolution in his writings but dissociates himself from it in practice in *Biedermann und die Brandstifter* (*The Fire-Raisers*, American title: *The Fire-Bugs*, 1957–58, premiere 1958 Schauspielhaus Zurich). It was this play which established Frisch's international reputation and which together with Dürrenmatt's *Der Besuch der alten Dame* re-established German-speaking nations as a force in world drama.

In *Biedermann* Frisch takes up again the question of the source of guilt. This was a theme he had also explored in a play somewhat similar to Dürrenmatt's *Die Ehe des Herrn Mississippi*—*Graf Öderland* (*Count Öderland*, premiere 1951 Schauspielhaus Zurich, directed by Steckel, rewritten 1956 and 1961). The title-figure is a respectable public prosecutor who escapes from the boredom of his bourgeois existence by leading a band of axe-swinging revolutionaries.

Somewhat less fantastic is the situation of *Biedermann*. Gottlieb Biedermann, a prosperous conformist bourgeois, is disturbed one evening by Schmitz, a homeless wrestler seeking shelter. Despite his fears that Schmitz might be a fire-raiser, he allows him to stay the night, asking his wife to throw him out in the morning. Playing on Frau Biedermann's sentimentality, Schmitz not only manages to remain in the house but also arranges for his companion, Willy Eisenring, to stay. When Biedermann can no longer ignore the fact that the two intruders really are fire-raisers, he sees his only salvation in currying their favour. He lies to the police about their activities and invites them to dine with him. At the end of the meal he hands over the matches with which they detonate the fuse to the barrels of petrol stored in the loft. In an epilogue written for the West German premiere (Städtische Bühnen Frankfurt, directed by Harry Buckwitz), Biedermann and his wife appear in Hell. It is a lightly written piece, more of a revue sketch than an amplification of the main play, in which Biedermann still does not recognise that he has done wrong, and the Chorus proudly proclaim that in the newly-built city the past has been forgotten:

> Completely cleared and forgotten the ruins,
> Completely forgotten all those too
> Whose remains were charred, their screams
> From the flames . . .
> Completely of the past are they.
> And silent.[11]

As Hellmuth Karasek has pointed out, while Dürrenmatt's plays end when the plot has taken its worst possible twist, Frisch's plays end where they began—with no-one any wiser than at the start.[12]

In this 'Morality Play without a Moral' Frisch presents a parable of the bourgeoisie's relationship to terrorism and political violence. While the theme was inspired by the Communist take-over of Czechoslovakia in 1948, it also has obvious references to the German middle-classes' contribution to the rise of Fascism. The willingness of Biedermann to tolerate the fire-raisers in his house is not due only to cowardice: he is also a master at self-deception. He cannot see the truth because he does not want to see it, any more than the Germans who supported Hitler took seriously the statements in *Mein Kampf* about the 'final solution of the Jewish problem'. As Willy Eisenring explains to Biedermann: 'the best and surest camouflage, I find, is still the plain, naked truth. Funnily enough. No-one believes it.'[13] So Biedermann thinks the truth is a joke and uses language as a means of distortion instead of as a means of communication. Thus when he says: 'My God, we must show a little trust, a little goodwill',[14] he is in fact eaten up by suspicion.

The play succeeds well, because despite the seriousness of its theme, it does not take itself too seriously. As a comic element it has a chorus of firemen, parodying the chorus of Greek tragedy and so undercutting the statement of the play—a typical expression of Frisch's scepticism about the value of his writing. In a parody of a chorus from Sophocles' *Antigone* the firemen sum up the play:

> Much is senseless, and nothing
> More senseless than this story:
> Which once set ablaze
> Killed many but not all
> And changed nothing.[15]

Frisch is being unnecessarily modest. There is nothing senseless about Biedermann's question to the audience: 'cross your heart, sirs, what would you have done, by God, if you'd been in my place? And when?'[16]

In his other major play, *Andorra* (1958–61, premiere 1961 Schauspielhaus Zurich, directed by Kurt Hirschfeld) Frisch goes further into the causes of Fascism, in particular of antisemitism. Here he reaches the end of a line of development that began with *Nun singen sie wieder*, in which each side had a fixed view of the enemy as devils. The same theme recurs in *Als der Krieg zu Ende war* (*When the War Was Over*, 1947–48, premiere 1949 Schauspielhaus Zurich), in which a woman hiding in the cellar of a house, which is occupied by Russian soldiers, discovers that the Russian colonel is not in fact a monster and willingly becomes his mistress. Although it is not concerned with war or minority groups, there is a similar consideration in *Don Juan oder Die Liebe zur Geometrie* (*Don Juan or The Love of Geometry*, 1952, premiere 1953 Schauspielhaus Zurich and Schiller-Theater Berlin). Here Don Juan is not the legendary lover but a man who prefers geometry to the company of women. An image has been imposed on him which bears no relationship to reality.

In a less comic manner *Andorra* deals with the same problem. Andri (the name is surely derived from the German word 'anders', meaning 'different') is in reality the illegitimate son of the Teacher, born to him by a woman from the neighbouring state of the 'Blacks'. Not wishing to lose his reputation for respectability, the Teacher pretends to his community that Andri is a Jewish foundling, whom he has saved from persecution by the antisemitic Blacks. As he grows up, Andri becomes the victim of prejudice. When he and his fellow Apprentice both make chairs, the Carpenter will not accept that Andri's chair is the sound one. He insists that Andri is responsible for the poorly made chair of the Apprentice and gives Andri a job as a salesman instead: 'everyone ought to do what's in their blood.'[17] Prejudice wins out over truth. When Andri seeks the hand of the Teacher's daughter, Barblin, in marriage, he is refused. Andri, not knowing that she is his half-sister, believes himself once again the victim of racial feeling. The Priest tries to comfort Andri by urging him to accept his Jewishness, when Andri's mother suddenly appears, motivated by somewhat belated maternal concern. The truth about Andri is thus revealed and the Priest now urges him to accept the fact that he is not really a Jew. But Andri can no longer escape from the image that others have imposed upon him. Finally the Blacks invade the country, and Andri is delivered up to them as a prisoner. In the last scene a grotesque 'Jew-inspection' takes place. Andri is recognised as a Jew from his gait and is led away by the Blacks. His father hangs himself, and Barblin, her head shaved as 'a Jew's whore', loses her sanity.

In the community of 'Andorrans' there are recognisable similarities with Frisch's own country. To a Swiss audience and to any public that prides itself on its supposed racial tolerance, it is shown convincingly that 'it could have happened here'. For a German audience there is something more familiar: the excuses and equivocations of the survivors, of those who must bear the guilt. In a device characteristic of Frisch's technique, each member of the community steps forward between scenes to defend his part in Andri's fate. Only the Priest admits his guilt: 'Thou shalt not make unto thee any graven image,'[18] he prays, confessing that he had made a 'graven image' of Andri. Typically it is the Doctor, the intellectual, whose testimony is the most disturbing:

> I admit we were all mistaken at the time, and that is something I can of course only deplore. How often must I repeat it? I'm not in favour of atrocities and never have been. . . . Anyway, I only saw the young man two or three times. As for the beating-up which is supposed to have occurred later, well I never saw it. All the same, I condemn it of course. I can only say it wasn't my fault, quite apart from the fact that his behaviour—I'm afraid you can't hide the fact—became more and more—let's be frank—Jewish in a way, although it may well be that the young man was an Andorran like the rest of us.[19]

It is clear that, just as Biedermann had learnt nothing, so the Andorrans will continue to indulge their prejudices.

Unfortunately, despite the quality of Frisch's play, there is no real analysis of antisemitism. Apart from the Doctor's complaint that all the university-chairs of the world are occupied by Jews, we are never given any insight into the sources of racial prejudice; we see only its manifestations. Furthermore, by making Andri in fact a Gentile, Frisch shows that the prejudice is here built on a fiction. This smacks very much of the liberal's attempt to seek racial harmony by denying any real cultural differences between ethnic groups, whereas harmony can be based only on genuine respect for such differences. Frisch is caught in a dilemma: as a humanist, he sees the dangers of petrifying individuals into fixed images; as a political thinker and as a dramatist it is his task to give his characters fixed roles.

It is therefore not surprising that after *Andorra* he abandoned playwriting for six years and that when he returned to the stage it was not with a political parable but—again similar to Dürrenmatt's development—with a very personal piece, as its title reveals: *Biografie. Ein Spiel* (*Biography. A Game*, 1967, premiere 1968 Schauspielhaus Zurich). Already Frisch had shown a debt to Pirandello in his repeated concern with role-playing; now in Pirandellian fashion he uses the flexibility of the stage to illuminate the possibilities of a human life. Kürmann, a behavioural scientist, is given the opportunity by a figure called the Recorder of turning back his life to any point and effecting any changes he desires. In a rather extreme attempt to escape from his unhappy marriage, Kürmann joins the Communist Party so that he will not be made Professor and will therefore not meet his future wife at the party held to celebrate his appointment. But despite his political affiliations he still ends up both as a professor and married. In this latest play of Frisch we see not only how once again everything ends as it began but also the strongest expression yet of his scepticism about the relevance of political commitment.

After Frisch, most plays that concerned themselves with Fascism and the war were documentary in nature. A number of others, however, took their lead from the retrospective comments of the characters in *Andorra* by examining how West Germany has come to terms with its past. In place of the question; how had respectable citizens become mass-murderers? a new one arose: how could former mass-murderers continue to lead normal lives as respectable citizens? Martin Walser (b. 1927), also well known as a novelist, displayed particular interest in this problem. In his essay on a new form of realism needed by the theatre, *Realismus X* (1964), he writes:

> I believe that every realistic portrayal of the Third Reich *must* reach up into our own times; it *must* expose the characters to the historical provocations of that period and show how those characters acted then and how they act today.[20]

His *Eiche und Angora* (*Rabbit Race*, 1962, premiere 1962 Schiller-Theater Berlin) is the first of the intended three parts of 'a German chronicle'. It displays Walser's formula of 'Realism X' partly in its style, which is a blend of naturalism and comic exaggeration, and partly in its theme. We witness German villagers in the panic of the last stages of the war, then five years later congratulating themselves on the wisdom of their surrender to the French who are now in occupation, and finally in 1960, during the period of West German rearmament, rejecting defeatist talk of surrender because they have a new 'enemy' in the East. Gorbach, the former Nazi official, shows himself remarkably adept at moving with the times. Only Alois, a simple-minded character who breeds rabbits, cannot keep pace. He had joined the Communist Party because he liked their songs and ended up being tortured and sterilised in a concentration camp. Desperately eager to change his ways, he becomes a staunch Nazi, but again finds himself in trouble when he retains his convictions longer than it is expedient for him to do so. Finally, after embarrassing the villagers once more, Alois is sent back to the local mental home.

Alois stands in contrast with Brecht's Schweyk. While Schweyk had undermined Nazi authority with a subtle lack of co-operation, Alois shows himself only too willing to join with the party in power. Walser's 'new realism' shows that the Nazis were not a manifestation of the devil, as Zuckmayer had suggested, but were the same sort of ordinary people, with all their selfishness and incompetence, as those who hold power in West Germany today. It is the wise fool Alois who reveals them for what they are.

The second part of the 'German chronicle' (the third has never appeared) was *Der schwarze Schwan* (*The Black Swan*, 1964, premiere 1964 Staatstheater Stuttgart, directed by Peter Palitzsch). While *Eiche und Angora* retained a comic approach which made the grotesque situation of Alois particularly disturbing, *Der schwarze Schwan* is characterised by an unrelieved gloom reminiscent of Kafka, on whom Walser had written his doctoral thesis in 1951. The setting is a psychiatric clinic, the head of which bears the ironical name Liberé. He is the former doctor of a concentration camp who pretends to his daughter that he spent the war years in India. He tries by every means to banish the past from his memory. So does his former colleague Goothein, whose son Rudi is brought to the clinic for treatment. Uncovering the guilt from which his father is trying to escape, Rudi takes his life. It is a meaningless suicide and yet Rudi's only way of ridding the burden of guilt which threatens to crush him; for one can only 'Pretend or forget . . . You can't take part.'[21] The weakness of the play is primarily due to the fact that it has lost its general relevance; it is not the chronicle of a nation but of a particular family of a very special kind. Significantly, Walser, like Dürrenmatt and Frisch, has turned from 'public' themes to domestic problems, as in *Die Zimmerschlacht* (*Home-Front*, premiere 1967 Kammerspiele Munich) and *Ein Kinderspiel* (*Child's Play*, premiere 1971 Staatstheater Stuttgart).

Another popular play which examined West German attitudes to the Nazi past was Hans Günter Michelsen's *Helm* (premiere 1965 Städtische Bühnen Frankfurt). The situation is almost a cross between *Waiting for Godot* and *Ten Little Niggers*. Five former German soldiers have just had a reunion with their former army-cook, Fritz Helm (the equivalent in English would be Tommy Helmet). They are now waiting for him in a clearing in the woods. It gradually emerges that they all shared the responsibility for Helm ending in a 'punishment battalion' where he had been badly wounded. One by one, the ex-officers' nerves crack and they run off into the woods. Each time, a shot is heard from the direction in which they have gone. Finally, Helm's old Division-Commander is left alone on stage, justifying the brutality and unfairness of his past before the unuttered reproaches of Helm. This projection of his own guilt onto a silent accuser recalls similar behaviour by the Emperor in Frisch's *Die chinesische Mauer*. And since we never learn whether Helm has in fact shot his former superiors or has perhaps just been playing a macabre game with them, the open ending throws out a question to the audience: are we not projecting our own notions of revenge onto Helm, who may after all not even be in the woods? Have we not betrayed our own sense of guilt?

Already these later dramas of 'Bewältigung der Vergangenheit' show in fact more concern with the German present than the German past. As this concern grew greater, so the foundations were laid for the development of political drama.

Notes to Chapter 5

1. *Tagebuch 1946–49*, Suhrkamp, Frankfurt, 1958, pp. 149–50.
2. *Stücke*, Vol. I, Suhrkamp, Frankfurt, 1962, p. 134.
3. *Wolfgang Borchert in Selbstzeugnissen und Bilddokumenten*, ed. Peter Rühmkorf, Rowohlt, Reinbek bei Hamburg, 1961, p. 40.
4. Cit. Rudolf Lange, *Carl Zuckmayer*, Friedrichs Dramatiker des Welttheaters No. 33, Velber bei Hannover, 2nd edn., 1973, pp. 43–44.
5. Zuckmayer, *Gesammelte Werke*, Vol. III, Fischer, Frankfurt, 1960, p. 522.
6. Ibid., p. 617.
7. Ibid., p. 606.
8. Ibid., p. 613.
9. *Gesammelte Werke*, Vol. IV, p. 196.
10. *Tagebuch 1946–49*, p. 285.
11. *Stücke* II, p. 344.
12. H. Karasek, *Max Frisch*, Friedrichs Dramatiker des Welttheaters No. 17, Velber bei Hannover, 5th edn., 1974, p. 14.
13. *Stücke* II, p. 128.
14. Ibid., p. 123.
15. Ibid., pp. 155–56. The same chorus from *Antigone* was parodied by Dürrenmatt at the end of *Der Besuch der alten Dame* and used by him in *Herkules und der Stall des Augias*.
16. Ibid., p. 140.
17. Ibid., p. 227.
18. Ibid., p. 254.
19. Ibid., p. 289.
20. M. Walser, 'Realismus X', *Deutsche Dramaturgie der Sechziger Jahre*, ed. Helmut Kreuzer, Max Niemeyer, Tübingen, 1974, p. 27.
21. *Theater 1964*, Friedrich, Velber bei Hannover, p. 79.

6 Political Theatre in the East

Although he died in 1956, having produced little new theoretical or creative work in the post-war years,[1] Bertolt Brecht (1898–1956) is still the single most important figure of contemporary German theatre. His has been the strongest influence on the development of political drama in Germany and in the whole world.

The focus of his post-war activities was the Berliner Ensemble, which he founded in 1949 with his wife, the Austrian-born actress Helene Weigel in what was then the Soviet Zone of East Berlin. First at the Deutsches Theater and then, after 1954, in the faded plush of the Theater am Schiffbauerdamm, Brecht could belatedly try out and revise the ideas he had spent much of his life propagating. This is a fact worth remembering when considering Brechtian theory: his propositions are to be tested and experimented with, there is no dogma in Brecht, and he himself constantly challenged his own thinking, even towards the end of his life rejecting the cherished term 'Epic Theatre' in favour of 'Dialectical Theatre.'

The Berliner Ensemble worked more as a team of scientists in pursuit of objective truth than as artists seeking aesthetic delights. A genuine collective was formed in which each participant's voice would be listened to and his views analysed and discussed; a scientific method was applied, whereby all those at a rehearsal had to make notes, enforcing on actors and directors alike the discipline of formulating their ideas in clear prose; the 'mystery' of the theatre was abandoned by allowing the public to attend rehearsals; above all, the Ensemble was united in one overriding aim, to make their theatre a force for social change:

> It is not enough to demand from the theatre insights, meaningful representations of reality. Our theatre must stimulate the pleasure of recognising truth and must organise the fun of changing reality. Our audience must not only hear how Prometheus bound is freed, but must school themselves in the joy of freeing him. All the skill and fun of the inventor or discoverer, all the triumphant feelings of the liberator must be taught by our theatre.[2]

Supported by generous subsidies from the East German government, the Berliner Ensemble boasts a company of some 60 actors and a total personnel of 250, enabling it to prepare its productions with elaborate care. It is common to devote over a hundred rehearsals to one production. The Wekwerth/Tenschert premiere of Brecht's *Die Tage der Commune* was rehearsed 212 times.

Brecht's first work in the post-war German theatre pre-dates the founding of the Berliner Ensemble. After running rings round the investigators of the Committee for Unamerican Activities he decided in 1947 to leave the United States for Switzerland. Here he was involved in two major productions of his own works: the premieres of *Herr Puntila und sein Knecht Matti (Mr. Puntila and His Man Matti)* and of *Antigone*.

The first of these, a *Volksstück* or play about the everyday life of common people, was written by Brecht in 1940–41 while in exile in Finland. It is based on a Finnish story of a man who is kindness himself when drunk, but who, once sober, is mean and uncompromising. As in *Der gute Mensch von Sezuan (The Good Woman of Setzuan* 1938–40) Brecht employs here a dialectical method which shows friendliness allied with degeneration and exploitation going hand in hand with prosperity. The spectator is challenged to seek the synthesis: the kind of society in which it is possible to be both friendly and prosperous, to have the *bonhomie* of the drunk without the attendant lethargy. *Puntila* was first performed in June 1948 at the Schauspielhaus, Zurich, directed by Kurt Hirschfeld with Brecht's assistance, with Leonard Steckel in the leading role. It was Steckel who again performed *Puntila* in the Brecht/Engel production with which the Berliner Ensemble officially opened the following year.

More important for Brecht's influence on the German theatre was the production a few months earlier of *Antigone*. It took place under the direction of Brecht and his designer Caspar Neher in the tiny Swiss town of Chur. Although Brecht's version of *Antigone*, which he had written after his arrival in Switzerland, does not compare favourably with his great plays of the late thirties and early forties, it is important in two respects: first, it established the working-pattern for Brechtian productions, secondly it is a good example of *Aneignung*, literally 'appropriation', a concept which has dominated the East German approach to classics since the war.

The initial motive for writing an *Antigone* derived from the need to find a challenging role for Helene Weigel for this, her first professional appearance since 1933, so that she might find a place in the German theatre again. Such practical considerations, as opposed to some rarefied literary inspiration, characterise Brecht's later work. Typically, he would not release scripts for publication until they had stood the test of rehearsal and performance.[3] So if we notice a certain lack of literary creativity in these post-war years, it is adequately compensated for by Brecht's well-documented practical work in the theatre.

In the case of *Antigone* he used a number of alienating devices: for example, Neher's bare stage with a rectangular acting area marked out with poles surmounted by horses' skulls, the use of primitive masks and the constant presence of all the actors who were invited to attend to their make-up or check their lines in full view of the audience. During rehearsal he trained his actors in 'epic' techniques, insisting on the overriding importance of the story which they, the actors, had the function of narrating. To this end he introduced *Brückentexte*, versified plot-summaries and stage-directions, which the performers were required to recite in rehearsal to assist them in maintaining a critical distance from their roles. Finally, he documented the production with comments and photographs, producing a *Modellbuch*, a published model not intended for slavish imitation, but—in the manner of scientists—offering the results of research on which the next ensemble might build. *Modellbücher* were subsequently published of all Brecht's major post-war productions.

Brecht's textual treatment of the original was typical: he plagiarised what was useful for his purposes, he rewrote the rest. Never one to share a bourgeois concept of ownership, Brecht had constantly pursued a policy of *Aneignung*, of appropriating from the past what might be put to use in the present. Conscious of both European and Asian traditions, he did not erect from them a museum for the imagination like Joyce, Pound or Eliot, but recreated them in living stories.

His version of *Antigone* is based on Hölderlin's translation from Sophocles. Bunge has shown that Brecht reproduced Hölderlin's text literally or almost literally in a fifth of his version and used a similar wording for a further third.[4] So skilful is Brecht's rewriting, that it is impossible to tell without reference to the original where Hölderlin ends and Brecht begins.

Despite the extent of his borrowings Brecht decisively shifts the emphasis of the original. In place of the traditional conflict between the uncompromising demands of political obedience and religious duty he shows 'the role of force used during the collapse of the political leadership' ('die Rolle der Gewaltanwendung bei dem Zerfall der Staatsspitze')[5] Antigone appears now not so much the loyal sister whose sacred duty it is to bury her brother, but as a representative of humanity who recognises too late the barbarism of the regime which she has condoned and to whose violence she now falls victim. In his 'rationalisation' ('Durchrationalisierung')[6] of the myth, Brecht therefore omits all references to the divine, except to the folk-god Bacchus, and the tragic figure of Creon becomes a power-drunk dictator: he is not waging a defensive war but is engaged in imperialistic aggression, attempting to seize the ore of Argos, and it is he, not Eteocles, that slays the fleeing Polyneices as a deserter.

This brutal figure of Creon naturally contains many elements of Hitler in his characterisation, and the allusions to the collapse of the Fascist dictatorship are reinforced by a Prologue set in Berlin at the end of the war. In this the sister of a deserter, who has been summarily executed by the SS, debates whether to risk her life by cutting him down from the meat-hook on which he has been hanged. Will she, like Antigone, have the courage to defy an unjust regime? The danger of using a contemporary allegory as in the Prologue is that paradoxically the audience may miss the relevance to their own situation. They must not be allowed to think that the threat implied by the figure of Creon was disposed of with the conquest of Nazism.[7]

It is here that we encounter one of the important principles of *Aneignung*. Brecht chose the figure of Antigone partly because of her 'historical distance' ('historische Entrücktheit')[8] and constantly reiterated the important assertion that such distance must be preserved in order that we may more objectively study the relevance of a historical situation for our own times. As Peter Palitzsch, one of Brecht's most distinguished pupils, put it:

> the stranger the period [of a play] appears to us, the greater its topicality. We say: aha—even then, when there wasn't any this or that or the other, the appropriate questions were being asked.[9]

If for no other reason than this, the historical drama of Brecht and his followers is more meaningful than that of any playwright discussed in Chapter 3.

What Brecht did here with *Antigone* was to become common practice in the Berliner Ensemble. They re-examined and adapted Goethe's *Urfaust* (1950), Lenz' *Der Hofmeister* (*The Tutor* 1950) Molière's *Don Juan* (1952), Farquhar's *The Recruiting Officer* (under the title of *Pauken und Trompeten*, 1954), culminating in their version of Shakespeare's *Coriolanus*. Brecht had begun work in 1951 on this, his first attempt to come face to face with Shakespeare, 'without whom a national theatre can hardly come into being'.[10] He abandoned work on the play, however, and it was the Ensemble in the course of 199 rehearsals under the direction of Manfred Wekwerth and Joachim Tenschert which finally completed it for its premiere in 1964. *Coriolan* must rank as one of the Berliner Ensemble's finer achievements and is a good example of the collective at work: Karl von Appen designed the set, Paul Dessau wrote the music, Ruth Berghaus rehearsed the fight-scenes, and Ekkehard Schall performed in the title-role, all major talents not submerged in the collective but rather given real scope to develop their gifts: 'They all unite their crafts in a joint undertaking without surrendering their independence.'[11]

Initially the Ensemble were unimpressed with Brecht's idea of reworking *Coriolanus*, but they were won over by his pointing out a 'printing-mistake' in the Folio edition. In the first scene of Shakespeare's play, Menenius calms the temper of a mutinous mob with his parable of the belly: he urges the citizens, the 'discontented members', to submit to the senators of Rome, 'this good belly', for it is from the belly that all nourishment and vigour proceed. At this point Coriolanus appears. Brecht suggested that the stage-direction for Coriolanus' entrance with his armed guard should in fact come *during* Menenius' speech: 'not the power of the word, but the word of power was to convince the Plebeians'.[12]

This initial 'correction' characterised the approach of the whole adaptation. The attempt was made to find a Marxist reading of the play relevant to contemporary society but which does not lose sight of the specific historical situation in which the play is set. In place of the mob's ingratitude towards Shakespeare's haughty and dynamic hero, Brecht put the tragedy of a great man's belief that he is indispensable:

> The tragedy of a single man naturally interests us much less than that of a community caused by a single man. At the same time we must remain close to Shakespeare if we are not going to mobilise his superior qualities against us. So it seems best for us to turn the hurt pride of Coriolanus into another significant attitude that is not too far removed from Shakespeare, namely Coriolanus' belief that

he cannot be replaced. It is this that leads to his destruction and robs the community of a valuable man.[13]

Two further comments by Wekwerth elucidate their intentions:

> In *Coriolan* we are not showing that heroes are replaceable, but we are showing a man who uses his irreplaceability to blackmail society and therefore *has to be* replaced.[14]

> The difference between Shakespeare and us is that for him the world is too base for a man like Coriolanus, and for us a man like Coriolanus is too costly for the world.[15]

In modern terms, the Berliner Ensemble version of *Coriolanus* destroys the 'personality cult' of Shakespeare's play and replaces it with a history seen unsentimentally from the point of view of the common man. But all this talk of ideological revision must not be allowed to obscure the fact that the Ensemble's production of *Coriolan*, with which they have achieved truly international success, is also very fine theatre. Although not wholly convinced by the interpretation, Peter Brook could write: 'In most respects, this version was a triumph. Many aspects of the play were revealed for the first time, much of it can seldom have been so well staged.'[16]

One example of the fine staging was the handling of the battle-scenes. Brecht had wanted to reduce these to one grand battle, but they were restored when it was felt that the Plebeians' faith in Coriolanus must gradually grow with his proven competence as a general. Consequently, the battles were not handled with noise and confusion but as terrifying rituals, in which Coriolanus appeared as the 'someone who had mastered the rules, as a specialist in slaughter.'[17]

What was also striking about the production was the awareness of the need for the fall of Coriolanus to be moving. It would have been both politically and theatrically ineffectual to portray the protagonist as some sort of villain, whose death would provide satisfaction. If there were still any need to put an end to the silly but widely-held belief that Brechtian productions must be unemotional, then one could point to Wekwerth's letter, written after the premiere to Ekkehard Schall, the actor who played Coriolanus. (How characteristic too that director and actor should continue to debate about the play after it has gone into performance!). Wekwerth writes:

> I'm still worried about Coriolanus' fall. You'll be surprised to hear that I find it too cold-blooded. If we take three hours to present and develop a character, his fall must cost something, for the spectator as well. In short, I miss the tragedy at this point.[18]

After developing this at some length, he sums up:

> I think we must carry the audience so far that they are deeply disturbed at the moment of his fall and feel pity for his inability to learn.[19]

There is no rejection of emotion; on the contrary, emotion is to be engendered, but directed to proper ends: the recognition that here a great man has been wasted, because his pride and the limited vision of the common people had seduced him into an inflated belief in his own importance.

Of the few new plays which Brecht wrote in the post-war years the most important was *Die Tage der Commune* (*The Days of the Commune*, 1948–49, premiere 1956 in Karl-Marx-Stadt directed by Benno Besson and Manfred Wekwerth). Already in 1936 during his exile in Scandinavia it is likely that he read Nordahl Grieg's play *The Defeat*, in which the Norwegian describes the fall of the Paris Commune of 1871. No doubt stimulated by the setting up of socialist states in Eastern Europe, especially in his own country, Brecht analyses the turbulent events of the Franco-Prussian war as a warning that idealism and revolutionary enthusiasm are not enough to ensure the victory of democracy:

BABETTE: To freedom! (. . .) Total freedom! . . .
LANGEVIN: (*smiling*) I'll drink to partial freedom! . . .
GENEVIEVE: Why partial freedom, Monsieur Langevin?
LANGEVIN: It leads to total freedom.
GENEVIEVE: And total, immediate freedom is an illusion?
LANGEVIN: In politics, yes.[20]

Typically, this theme is explored from the point of view not only of the Communards themselves but even more of the common people they represent. Of the fourteen scenes, only three deal with those in high places, showing the bourgeoisie betraying the Commune to appease German demands; four describe the setting-up of the Commune and their debate about the use of force to meet threats from outside; but half the scenes, the remaining seven, are set in the Rue Pigalle, where the wider issues are reflected on a domestic level in the family and friends of Madame Cabet. So we see Madame Cabet forced by circumstances to demand money from her lodger, who is himself penniless because he has not received his pay from the National Guard. While the bourgeoisie act with cynicism and the Communards talk with idealism, the common people are united by their empty pockets and empty stomachs: 'Education begins with eating!'[21]

The style of the play is less obviously epic than many of Brecht's and the Berliner Ensemble production in 1962 surprised many critics with its simple realism. Nevertheless the essential dialectic is strongly present. As Wekwerth, who directed it with Joachim Tenschert, stated: 'We made it a principle that we should only criticise what we at least also admired.'[22] The Commune and its revolution are therefore not idealised, its blundering and innocence are laid bare, but the audience is also made aware that men of such far-seeing ideals 'did more for human dignity in only 73 days than all the old regimes in eight centuries.'[23] Like Aristotle's prescription for the tragic hero, the Communards are neither wholly good nor wholly bad, and the sense of waste is the stronger for that.

Central to the future of the Commune is their debate about the use of force. As idealists they must abandon the terrorisation practised by former governments, as political realists they recognise they must defend with force what has been achieved. Since the Commune fails and the Cabet family meet a bloody death because of the pacifistic decision of the Commune, Brecht might seem to imply that force must be used to meet force. Indeed, some Western critics took the production to be an expression of approval of the Berlin Wall or even an incitement to attack Western Germany. But Brecht also offers very strong arguments against force, arguments which win over the majority of the sympathetically portrayed Communards. As usual, the audience are treated as adults and asked to decide for themselves: is it possible to defend the revolution against outside aggression without compromising its ideals? It was a prophetic question that Brecht and many others had to face after the uprising in East Germany on 17 June, 1953.

In addition to performing Brecht's own plays and adapting classics, the Berliner Ensemble also gave encouragement to East German writers. They produced a play about the battle for Moscow by one of East Germany's leading poets, Johannes R. Becher's *Winterschlacht* (*Winter Battle*, 1941, premiere 1942 by the Heinrich Heine Club in Mexico). Although Brecht and Wekwerth experimented with it in 1954, it was not finally performed until 1959, possibly because of Brecht's dissatisfaction with the presentient and optimistic view in the play that German soldiers had seen through the Nazi lie as early as 1941. A play that did achieve performance under Brecht's personal supervision was Erwin Strittmatter's *Katzgraben* (1953, premiere 1953 by Berliner Ensemble at the Deutsches Theater Berlin). It was written for amateurs in 1951 and revised on the suggestion of Brecht.

Reminiscent of the Prologue to *Der kaukasische Kreidekreis* (*The Caucasian Chalk Circle* 1943–45), it deals with the dispute between old and young farmers about the building of a road. It is only when the tractors roll into the village at the end of the play that all the farmers begin to understand the social change they are involved in.

Another *Zeitstück*, or play dealing with a contemporary problem, which was written in collaboration with the Berliner Ensemble, was Helmut Baierl's *Frau Flinz* (1961, premiere 1961 by the Ensemble under the direction of Wekwerth and Palitzsch). It is in a sense a reply to Brecht's *Mutter Courage*. While Mother Courage learns nothing from her experiences and trundles her cart off into the war at the end of the play, Frau Flinz finally accepts that she is living in a new society to which she must adapt. This new society is the emergent Socialist Germany of the immediate post-war years, and against this society she initially operates to further her own self-interest with all the resourcefulness of Mother Courage and the cunning of Schweyk. But Baierl and his collaborators are at pains to show that her self-interest and that of the new state in fact coincide, a recognition to which Frau Flinz herself finally comes.

In the reform of Flinz and of the farmers in *Katzgraben* lies the weakness of many post-war East German plays. The happy end may be good propaganda, but it is poor dialectics. The resolution is achieved on the stage and not in the mind of the spectator. In place of the repeated challenges issued by Brecht's work, we see too often the self-congratulation which has now led the East German theatre into something of an impasse.

This is one reason why Brecht's most important follower in the East is Peter Hacks. Born in Breslau in 1928, he studied in Munich and in 1955 became one of the few theatre people to migrate from West to East. (Until the erection of the Wall in 1961 most movement was in the other direction). He worked with the Berliner Ensemble and became

Dramaturg at the Deutsches Theater. Since 1963 he has lived as a free-lance writer in East Berlin.

Hacks too has written propagandistic *Zeitstücke*, the plots of which sound like parodies of Socialist Realist drama, e.g. *Die Sorgen und die Macht* (*Anxiety and Power* 1960, premiere 1960 in Senftenberg, second version 1962 Deutsches Theater Berlin), which deals with the production problems of a briquette factory. In the First Act the factory has produced more briquettes than its target, but they are of poor quality. In the Second Act the quality is restored but there is a drop in the number produced. As a result one of the leading workers becomes sexually impotent. So he joins The Communist Party, makes improvements in the factory, and both productivity and quality are achieved—as is the return of his potency!

Like many plays of this type, it is difficult to take seriously. And this is precisely Hacks' point, a point which was not well received by the authorities who required a rewriting before it could be performed in Berlin. The same difficulties were encountered by *Moritz Tassow* (1964, premiere 1965 Volksbühne, East Berlin) which is set in an idyllic East German village in 1945. Written in blank verse, it tells of a dumb swineherd who finds his tongue after reading Marx. He leads a revolution and seizes the property of the local landowner with improbable ease. But the disorganised rebellion fails: 'Politics is only possible without people',[24] Tassow complains, and it is left to the sober party-functionary, Mattukat, to sort out the mess and form a collective. Tassow goes off, declaring he will become

> A writer, sir, that is the only job
> Where I am not obliged to seek for men
> Who understand or wish to follow me.[25]

Although this play is set in 1945, the whole idiom is that of a bucolic idyll: the mention of a telephone seems like an anachronism in this pastoral of pipe-playing swineherds. Most of Hacks' plays have historical themes, which are better suited to the chap-book characters of his style. Indeed his first drama reveals this in the title: *Das Volksbuch von Herzog Ernst oder Der Held und sein Gefolge*, (*The Chap-Book of Duke Ernest or The Hero and His Followers*, 1953, premiere 1967 Nationaltheater, Mannheim). In the Holy Roman Empire of the tenth century Ernst passes through a series of Candide-like misfortunes, with the essential difference that he, unlike Candide, always has a loyal follower or two to die or suffer on his behalf. When his feudal retinue is finally exterminated, he returns to the Emperor's court where he wreaks vengeance on the originator of his troubles.

Die Eröffnung des indischen Zeitalters (*The Introduction of the Indian Epoch*, 1954, premiere 1955 Kammerspiele, Munich, revised for publication under the title, *Columbus*) describes Christopher Columbus' attempts to convince the Spanish court of the feasibility of finding a Western sea-route to the Indies. His interests are those of a scientist, but he finds that instead of introducing a new 'Indian Epoch', he has become the unwitting instrument of exploiting colonialism:

> This Indian epoch, this age of gold, this age of greed, does not seem to be that age of reason and virtue which by imagining it, lent my

soul such conforting strength . . . Obviously, it has hardly any advantages, except that it is new.[26]

Perhaps Hacks' best play to date is *Die Schlacht bei Lobositz* (*The Battle of Lobositz*, 1954, premiere 1956 Deutsches Theater Berlin). This battle was the first confrontation of the Seven Years' War between Prussia and Austria. Based on a contemporary autiobiography, events are seen mainly from the viewpoint of a young Swiss, Ulrich Braeker, who has been press-ganged into Prussian service and finally deserts. Despite the clarity with which it is shown that only the gentry benefit from the war and that the poor are always the losers, it takes Braeker all three acts to arrive at the firm decision to desert. This is because he suffers from 'a propensity to subordination' and all too readily forgives the treacherous Lieutenant who press-ganged him. This Lieutenant Markoni sets out to prove to his fellow-officers that love for one's men will achieve more abiding loyalty and better results on the battle-field than the traditional method of making the common soldier more afraid of his own officers than of the enemy. (There are unmistakable echoes here of the 'civilians in uniform' concept, propagated in West Germany in 1954, when the play was written, as an attempt to sugar the pill of rearmament). In a brilliantly conceived scene, Markoni shows his tenderness towards Braeker by combing and powdering his hair while assuring him that master and servant should work together for the same ends, because this will assure the prosperity of both. In conclusion he lays a cloth over Braeker's face and envelops him in a mist of powder. But the conscript does not remain blinded for long; he has the sense to desert and refuses to save Markoni from captivity on learning that his master had intended to place him on the battle-field where he was bound to get killed, the most effective means of preventing desertion. On seeing his former master wounded and in chains, Braeker exclaims: 'Then I regard the case of the poor man from Tockenburg, my case, as remarkable: for it is a case of justice achieved in this world.'[27]

Hacks' next play was set in the same period. *Der Müller von Sanssouci* (*The Miller of Sanssouci*, 1955, premiere 1958, Kammerspiele, Deutsches Theater Berlin) is based on a well-known anecdote about Frederick the Great, which Brecht had contemplated using as an idea for a comedy. The story goes that Frederick had tried to prevent a miller from grinding his corn near the royal palace of Sanssouci, because the noise disturbed the affairs of state. The miller boldly replied: 'There are still judges in Berlin'. All of which was meant to prove that in the Prussian state King and commoner were equal before the law. The twist that Hacks introduces is that the King urges the miller to utter his courageous words as a public-relations exercise. Even so, because like Braeker the miller willingly bows before authority, Frederick has to resort to physical force to induce his too loyal subject to perform. When the miller finally chokes out the words: 'There are still judges in Berlin', Frederick, 'extraordinarily moved', comments: '. . . only amongst these people could I become what I am.'[28] Feeling himself in favour with the King, the miller seeks the release of his servant from conscription. The King enquires whether he has been recruited according to the law. He has, and of the course the King has no power to change the law. This 'sting in the tail' suggests that however benevolent the despot may be, it is the laws, the institutions that must be changed.

His most recent historical piece, *Margarete in Aix* (1965–66, premiere 1969 Basler Theater) returns to the Middle Ages and to blank verse. Margaret, Queen of England, exiled at her father's court in Provence, looks to the support of Charles the Bold to wage war on Edward III. But Charles is defeated in battle by Swiss peasants and Margaret dies from sheer chagrin. She joyfully envisages the shock her death will cause, but in fact her body is discovered during a banquet and, so as not to disturb the jollifications, a courtier dances with her corpse. He finally conceals it in an instrument-case on which later the Provence is signed away to Louis XI. Although we do not have such a clear sense in this play that history is made by the common people, at least the grotesque irony of Margaret's fate is a demonstration of the powerlessness of the great before the movement of history.

As well as seeking political themes in history, Hacks has also found them in myth. He adapted Aristophanes' *Peace*, (*Der Frieden*, 1962, premiere 1962 Deutsches Theater, Berlin), which already in the original shows the common peasants and not the rulers releasing Peace from the well in which she was trapped. Benno Besson's production of *Der Frieden* created something of a record in Hamburg on its 1965 tour when it was greeted by applause lasting three-quarters of an hour.

Another record has been achieved by Hacks' *Amphitryon* (1967, premiere Deutsches Theater, Göttingen). After Dürrenmatt's *Play Strindberg*, it has been the second most frequently produced contemporary play in Germany over the last ten years (46 productions in the West alone). It is easy to see why it has been popular with theatre managements: it satisfies both the conservative demand for something entertaining and 'classical' and the progressive demand for a political play by a living German author. It is not easy at first to see in what sense the play is political, since it fairly closely follows the myth as treated by Plautus, Molière, Kleist and Giraudoux. Jupiter, having fallen in love with Alcmene, assumes the form of her husband, Amphitryon, to seduce her. When Amphitryon returns from the wars, a predictable series of comic confusions result, until Jupiter reveals his true nature and returns to the heavens. There are two main shifts of emphasis in Hacks' blank-verse retelling of the story. First, just as in *Columbus* the hero is dumbfounded to find everyone—except the academics—agreeing that the earth is round, so here much of Jupiter's effort is wasted because Alcmene accepts him as a god long before he has revealed the fact. Secondly, the traditional ending in which Jupiter announces that Alcmene will give birth to Hercules is abandoned; instead his gift to her is the awareness of the heights to which her relationship with Amphitryon might soar. As I say, it is not immediately clear in what sense this is political. To be sure, there are the references to the unjust treatment of servants:

Now that is what's so true to life about
The ancient comedies, that smaller roles
Get all the beatings.[29]

There is also the critique of Amphitryon who imagines that success as a

54

warrior, public recognition and wealth are what give man his human dignity. But the axis of the play is love, and it is here that we must look. Constantly the rigid behaviour of the husband, Amphitryon, is contrasted with the burning passion of the lover, Jupiter. To Jupiter's astonished question: 'But don't men love at all?', Mercury replies: 'Oh yes, at times, But always briefly, as it wears them out.'[30] By contrast, Jupiter tells Alcmene: 'The few short hours that love can lend man greatness/Will justify the whole of his existence.'[31] This in itself might be yet another romantic celebration of love, but it acquires broader meaning towards the end, when Jupiter is speaking of the creation of the world:

> Yet when it was created,
> An error came to light: the world was.
> It was just as it was and nothing else.
> Signed and sealed and delivered. Matter was
> No longer in love, it had been married off.
> And now the only force that can transform
> The fossil frame of habits we call laws
> Into the reckless play of happy chance
> Is Chaos' daughter, love.[32]

Like the new universe envisioned by Brecht's Galileo in which the earth moves round the sun, the old laws are overturned and everything is set in motion, Jupiter's lesson of love has serious implications for man:

> A husband is not a lover ...
> And man in what he does and does not do
> May be excused by necessity. Don't say
> Though you're excused and therefore free from guilt.
> You who are finite, did you never yearn
> Towards infinity? You who can never
> Achieve so many things, can you not sense
> The loss of that which lies beyond your reach?
> You have your limits. Yet to recognise
> They're there means crossing them. Oh man, man, man,
> Don't take your faults for granted nor take the standard
> With which you judge yourself from your own self,
> That's what your love towards Alcmene would
> Have taught you, had you been able to be taught.[33]

When Amphitryon presses Jupiter to say clearly how one may unite 'beauty without strength, and strength without beauty', Mercury conveniently summons him away on heavenly business. No divine programme is forthcoming, but a Utopian vision is projected. It is for each spectator to find his self-transcending renewal in love, and it is in this sense that Hacks clearly regards loving as a political act, as in his most recent play, *Adam und Eva* (1973). The dictatorships which through history have consistently sought to repress sexuality would agree with him.

From this examination of Hacks' plays, it is clear how much he owes to Brecht, at whose feet he went to sit in 1955. From Brecht above all he derived the conviction that the theatre is a political institution, even if he casts doubt on the significance of the writer, as we see in Tassow's departing words or in the ironical figures of the troubadours in *Margarete in Aix*. As a political institution, the theatre must look at the present and the past, historical and mythical, not for psychological studies of individuals but to trace the movements of history which bring about social change. So we see the dialectical process at work—between scientific idealism and colonial exploitation in *Columbus*, between laws in the service of the common man and those that serve the rulers in *Der Müller von Sanssouci*, and most frequently of all that between the world as it could be and the world as it is (*Die Schlacht bei Lobositz, Moritz Tassow, Amphitryon*). History is seen through the eyes of the ordinary people who make it, not the so-called leaders who imagine they are controlling affairs (Columbus the weaver, Braeker the cowherd, the Miller, the peasants in *Der Frieden*). Typically, the scene in *Die Schlacht bei Lobositz* in which we learn of the outcome of the battle is the shortest in the play with five spoken words: 'Messieurs, la bataille est gagnée.'[34] After all, it really does not matter which side has won, certainly not to the fallen and little enough to the survivors. And speaking of survivors, we recognise in characters like Herzog Ernst, Columbus and Braeker the ability to trace a naive and flexible path of survival through the complexities of existence like their literary forbears, Schweyk and Galileo.

In seeking the relevance of history and myth, Hacks also follows Brecht in avoiding the error of updating the material and so wrenching it out of its historical context. As Hacks said, 'You have to leave Athens in Ancient Greece'[35] and however stylised the action or characters, the plays remain essentially true to their period. This paradox that the unfamiliar and not the familiar reveals reality had been stated in a note by Brecht: 'Our theatre lives, if it is to live at all, from the unexpected, the surprising, the remarkable. Yes, from touches (*Pointen*) that provide reality.'[36] One of many 'touches' that distinguish Hacks' work comes in the last scene of *Die Schlacht bei Lobositz*. Braeker is haggling with an Austrian captain over the price of some bread and meat, claiming he has only one groschen left in the world. His fellow Swiss deserters whom he has not seen for some while suddenly appear and offer him money. Does he forget his purchases in his joy at seeing his long-lost companions? Does he eagerly accept the offer of money, so that he can complete his bargaining? Not at all. His reaction is: 'You idiots, you're ruining the prices.'[37] He gets what he wants on favourable terms and only then greets his friends. It is the least expected of the three possibilities, but—for a peasant at a time of hardship—by far the most real.

This is an alienating moment, one which makes us look at reality with new eyes. It is a device which Hacks uses freely to prick the bubble of uncritical involvement, often effectively at the start of a play. 'You, sacred hearth aglow beneath the ash ...' begins a masked figure in flowing robes as the curtain rises on *Amphitryon*. The audience settles in its seats recognising the familiar idiom of Germano-Greek drama—with a grunt of pleasure or a groan of dismay according to taste. But not for long. After seven lines of flowing iambic pentameters the actor stops: 'A stupid text, I don't like saying it.'[38] He turns out to be Jupiter rehearsing the part of Amphitryon, but on another level he is the actor inviting the audience to adopt a critical stance towards what it sees.

The structure of the plays is also Brechtian. There are the episodic scenes, not one scene sliding smoothly into another but jumping from incident to incident, not the inevitability of a wound-up spring but the repeatedly implied question: need this continue? Could the play not end here or take a different course? Indeed, this characteristic is responsible for the one structural flaw in *Die Schlacht bei Lobositz*. The first two acts are tightly constructed, but once Braeker has begun to desert, the play could end, and the almost random incidents of Act Three seem like an appendage (indeed two of them were cut in the West Berlin premiere in 1966). Another structural device which is familiar from Brecht is the introduction of songs. A particularly derivative example is that of the invalids who sing before the Battle of Lobositz to the accompaniment of a barrel-organ.

In this song as elsewhere, a debt to Brecht's linguistic style can also be seen. Like his master, Hacks displays a great range, from the poetry of *Amphitryon* or *Omphale* (1970, premiere 1970 Städtische Bühnen, Frankfurt) to the extreme economy of the colloquial dialogue in his history plays. Two examples from *Die Schlacht bei Lobositz* must suffice: observe the contraction and rhythmic balance of: 'An einer Kuh hängt, wer versteht, sie melken, dass sie Milch gibt.'[39] The literal translation is: 'To a cow is attached, he who understands, to milk it, that it gives milk', meaning: 'The man who knows how to milk a cow so that it will give milk is the one who learns to value it.' It is not often that an English sentence requires twice as many words to express the sense of one in German! The second example is a simple statement of love with a hauntingly rhythmic antithesis: 'Den, wenn ich lieben könnt, könnt ich lieben'[40] ('Him I could love, were I able to love').

Perhaps all these remarks have given the impression, by no means uncommon, that Hacks is a mere imitator of Brecht, but there are two major differences.

The first is that although there are a few Utopian elements in Brecht like the 'golden age almost of justice' under the wise judgments of Az-dak, most of his plays end pessimistically: Azdak himself must flee for his own safety, Shen-Te receives no answer from the gods and Galileo is full of self-reproach. As we have seen, Hacks' plays end with almost consistent optimism. It is not that he would wish us to believe that life is a Utopia; on the contrary we are constantly reminded to examine our lives and our society to see where we fail to achieve what is so desirable. Braeker may go happily on his way, the Miller may be able to continue grinding corn, but we do not forget to ask why the war or the threat to a man's livelihood were there in the first place.

Secondly, and this is in accord with the idyllic nature of the plots, there is a charm and grace about Hacks' writing which looks quite rococo beside Brecht's style. One sometimes has the impression of a Feydeau employed by the Berliner Ensemble. Indeed, in his wit and ebullient good humour Hacks will not spurn knockabout humour or simple farce, based for example on one of the oldest stage-jokes, the confusions caused by a failure to understand a foreign tongue (as between Columbus and the natives or Braeker and the Finns). We also find elements of the grotesque far beyond anything in Brecht. There is the corpse of Margaret being given a turn on the floor during a Provençal banquet, and when one dying soldier on the battle-field of

Lobositz asks another to give him his hand, the latter obliges by tossing over his severed hand.

In Hacks' attempts to return to the popular language, idyllic settings and exciting incident of the chap-book we recognise a highly intellectualised attempt to create the naive. This is exactly what Brecht sought to do and sometimes it really shows through. There is a scene in *Die Mutter* (*The Mother* 1930–32) in which the workers are learning to read and Pelagea Wlassowa enthusiastically says: 'The E in "Exploitation" is the same as the E in "Employee"'.[41] This patronising view of the illiterate worker makes me wince, but it must be admitted that most of the time Brecht is great enough to bring together his fine intellect and his childlike love of play. Hacks is not as great but has ventured onto similarly treacherous ground. When his writing is at its best, we enjoy playing his game of being shrewd but simple peasants and workers. All too often though the charade is puffed away and we end up in the world of J. M. Synge[42] at his worst, amidst a motley crew of rustics uttering their folksy sayings and doing their folksy deeds.

Despite these reservations, Hacks is the most successful playwright living in either German Republic and probably also the most talented. It is therefore surprising that he is almost totally unknown in Britain: I have been unable to trace any translations of his plays into English and am unaware of any stage-productions here. There may be political prejudice, but it seems unlikely with a playwright who has been more honoured in West Germany than in the East. More important are the factors that his plots are often related to specifically German interests (Prussian militarism, GDR production problems) and that his plays frequently require a cast of over twenty, a profligacy normally only granted to Shakespeare on the British stage. Most telling, however, are two further considerations: first, his language is highly concentrated and evocative, poetic in fact. Remembering Robert Frost's definition that poetry is what gets lost in translation, it is understandable that translators have shied away from the task of doing justice to Hacks (my own attempts should be indication enough of this). Secondly, as we have seen, Hacks owes a great deal to Brecht, and one can imagine that if a British theatre decides to tackle a Brechtian play it will normally turn to Brecht himself. Understandable as this situation is, it is nevertheless reprehensible that lesser talents like Hochhuth are known to English audiences, while Hacks remains neglected.

Besides Hacks the only other major East German playwright is Heiner Müller (The promising Ulrich Plenzdorf will be considered in Chapter 9). Born in 1929, Müller[43] worked for some years as journalist and editor, until at the age of 30 he devoted himself to full-time writing. He specialises in adaptations of classics and *Zeitstücke* with which he has repeatedly come into conflict with the East German authorities.

Examples of his *Zeitstücke* are: *Der Lohndrücker* (*Lowering the Wages*, 1956–57, premiere 1958 Städtische Theater Leipzig), *Die Korrektur* (*The Correction*, 1957, premiere 1958 Maxim-Gorki Theater Berlin), *Die Umsiedlerin oder Das Leben auf dem Lande* (*Change of Residence or Life in the Country*, 1956–61, premiere 1961 by students of the College of Economics Berlin-Karlshorst), *Der Bau* (*The Building-Site*, 1963–65) and *Zement* (*Cement*, 1973, premiere 1973 Berliner Ensemble).

Die Umsiedlerin and *Der Bau* have had no professional productions in the East, although Besson rehearsed *Der Bau* for a while before yielding to pressure to abandon the project. The official reason for Müller's disfavour was the accusation of 'formalism', an ill-defined term used to describe any art that does not conform to Social Realism. But the content of his plays surely also contributed to his difficulties, and the recent acceptance of his *Zement* is probably mainly due to the fact that it is based on a respected novel by the Russian Gladkov. *Der Lohndrücker*, for example, recently revived at the Schaubühne am Halleschen Ufer Berlin, describes the dilemma of a factory-worker who during the Nazi period had denounced a fellow-worker as a member of the Resistance. Some years after the war the informer and his victim, now a party-secretary, are back at the same factory. When the worker discovers a 'Western saboteur', the question arises: should he once more denounce a fellow worker? The party-secretary advises him that he should. As with Frau Flinz, he must recognise that the social system has changed and that the wrong course of yesterday is the right way of today. All ideologically sound, one might have thought, but the harshness of Müller's play, like Brecht's *Die Massnahme* (*The Measures Taken*, 1930), is not the kind of image the Communist Party likes to project. Such things may happen, but they are best not talked about.

Virtually an outcast after 1958, the year of publication and performance of *Der Lohndrücker*, Müller significantly wrote his next play about the exiled figure of Philoctetes, *Philoktet* (1958–65, premiere 1968 Residenztheater Munich). Philoctetes was the Greek who had been abandoned by Odysseus on the Isle of Lemnos, until a prophecy declared that Troy could not be conquered without his aid. Odysseus and Neoptolemos therefore return to persuade him to come to Troy. Philoctetes refuses until, in Sophocles' original, Heracles conveniently appears to command him to rejoin the Greek army.

In Müller's version it is not Philoctetes' miraculous bow that is needed but he himself is required to lead his disaffected troops against Troy. When he refuses, there can be no *deus ex machina* to solve the problem; instead Neoptolemos swiftly kills Philoctetes, and Odysseus concocts a story to tell in Troy that it was Trojans that had slain Philoctetes. The point again is made that means must justify the ends, that when great issues are at stake, force and lies are sometimes unavoidable. When Neoptolemos objects: 'As helper I am here, but not as liar', Odysseus snaps: 'But we require a helper here who lies.'[44]

Once more this play failed to find official favour and its only East German production to date has been by the students of the Karl Marx University Leipzig under the direction of Bernhard Scheller. Although Müller lives in East Berlin, it is in the West that he has had most success, particularly with his many adaptations. In these the ideologically justified brutality of his earlier plays has become more and more gratuitous. In his version of *Macbeth* (1971, premiere 1972 Brandenburg) bloody incidents proliferate, making Shakespeare's original seem tame by comparison. Angered by being made to wait by the drunken porter, Lennox chops off his leg; Banquo is castrated after his murder and Lady Macbeth amuses herself by seeing peasants tortured. For the Basle production Hollmann resourcefully used a giant disposal unit centre stage as a means of clearing away the many corpses. The world may be a violent place, but such unanalytical celebration of violence is not only distasteful; it is also pointless.

Both Hacks and Müller have experienced political difficulties, and in Müller's case it has no doubt accorded him undeserved prominence in the West. In Western democracies free speech, like free elections, is usually considered one of the cornerstones of an acceptable society. In the democracies of the East there is more concern with educating the public towards a Socialist awareness. It is as meaningless for a Communist state to allow many political viewpoints to be propagated as it would be for children to be taught many different forms of mathematics. Unfortunately, political truths can never be as objective or as verifiable as mathematical ones.

East Germany has the particular problems of being a country with little experience of democracy and of bordering on a capitalist state whose former claims to national sovereignty seemed to represent a real threat to survival. Understandably, its censorship has been even stricter than that of many other Communist states. There is no 'fringe' theatre and virtually no aesthetic experimentation such as one finds in the Absurd Theatre of Czechoslovakia or Grotowski's work in Poland. With a gain in self-assurance through international diplomatic recognition and economic prosperity there are now signs that official oversight of the theatres is relaxing from the stern measures passed by the 11th Plenum of the Central Committee of the SED (Socialist Unity Party) in 1965. In a recent issue of the East German monthly *Theater der Zeit* Peter Hacks could be rude not only about Brecht but even about amateur theatre in the trades unions, something that would simply not have got into print a few years ago.

The typical repertory of an East German theatre does not differ greatly from that of the West: here too the theatre is a museum for works of world drama, many of them of course originating in Eastern Europe. The major difference is in the presentation. Eschewing both antiquarian reconstructions and gimmicky re-interpretations, the principles of *Aneignung* are followed. Shakespeare, for example, is performed in such a way as to bring out the social and economic background of his plays, specifically the emergence of the Elizabethan bourgeoisie from the feudalism of the Middle Ages. Initially providing stimulating insights for those unfamiliar with a dialectical interpretation of the classics, the repeated application of the same analysis can easily become routine and ultimately lead to an impoverishment of world drama. The bourgeois theatre of the West may all too easily abandon its role as a political force, to the point where Max Frisch can say that nothing at all would change if all the theatres in the world were locked and the keys thrown in the river. On the other hand, the tendency in the East to justify the theatre in political terms leads to a narrowing of vision.

But what political statements can be made by the East German theatre? Understandably proud of the accomplishment of a social revolution which has ended poverty and unemployment, the German Democratic Republic all too readily celebrates its achievements, considers the revolution already quite finished and sees progress only in terms of increased productivity. In these circumstances the theatre has almost nowhere to go. It cannot—and does not want to—challenge the foundations of Socialist society; it can celebrate the overcoming of the capitalist past or it can portray the capitalist present, like the plays of Tennessee Williams, in a spirit of relief that such problems are not the problems of the Socialist state.

It may all be very salutary, but it is not very dynamic. The situation of East German theatre is close to that of Ulrich Plenzdorf's Edgar in *Die neuen Leiden des jungen W* (*The New Sorrows of the Young W*):

> No reasonably intelligent person can be against Communism nowadays. But otherwise they're against it. Perhaps you shouldn't take that so seriously. You don't need to be brave to be for it. But everyone wants to be brave. So they're against it. That's the way it is.[45]

The theatre wants to be brave but has no desire to challenge its society. For it is a society in a period of consolidation which is sensitively guarding its hard-won achievements; so the theatre can only lead from behind, and there is general talk of stagnation in the green rooms of East Germany.

The situation is not improved by the superb working conditions of the East German actor. After two years training in one of the state schools and two further years in a studio attached to a larger theatre, his career is assured for life. It is almost impossible to be dismissed from an ensemble, unless there has been a very flagrant breach of contract. It is by no means unknown for an altercation between director and actor to be cut short by the actor's offer to withdraw. After all, his wages will not be affected whether he performs or not. From Professor Kayser, the *Chefintendant* of the Leipzig theatres, I was interested to learn of his envy of the spirit prevalent amongst British actors, whose attitude is conditioned by a 'struggle for survival'. While Kayser sensibly enough had no desire to exchange the thoroughly humane treatment of the actor in East Germany with the jungle existence of his British counterpart, he saw only too clearly the dangers of coddling the profession. Hans Daiber's comment on the subsidised theatre of West Germany might equally apply here: 'Not only are the competent made more competent, but the incompetent are also made care-free and powerful.'[46]

For all its drawbacks, the East German theatre is a more consistently democratic institution than that in the other three German-speaking nations. The ensemble is represented in all decisions regarding management, appointments and choice of plays, and the *Intendant* is regarded as the leader of a collective rather than as a manager. Since he carries ultimate responsibility for the working of the collective, he is theoretically free to ignore the recommendations of the ensemble, but in practice he would be foolish to do so.

The East German theatre has also succeeded in fulfilling the pipe-dream of so many Western *Intendanten*: to bring the working-classes into the theatre. In Klaus Pfützner's survey in *Theater der Zeit* in August 1969 it was shown that 20 to 30% of audiences were of working-class background, and the proportion has certainly increased since then. Admittedly, much of this is on paper rather than in fact, since the tickets may have been sold to workers who then fail to attend the actual performance. A theatre can be 'sold out' and yet be full of empty seats—not surprising when one considers that most East German workers begin their day at 6 a.m.!

Despite these qualifications it is still impressive to see how receptive the working-class is to their theatre. It has been due to a slow process of education, well organised distribution of season-tickets through trades union organisations and to colossal subsidies. Subsidies in the East are even more generous than those in the West: for each theatre seat the state pays on average 8.– MDN (about £1.50 at the official exchange rate), which represents a subsidy of about 90%. It is still possible to see a play for 1 Mark (under 20p). Moreover, unlike the West, East German theatres are not called upon to justify their subsidies in terms of public success.

Now that the great days of the Berliner Ensemble are past and even Besson's productions have lost their bite, the East German theatre is healthy but unexciting. One is reminded of Galileo's image of the oyster in Brecht's play: it is only the unhealthy oyster that produces the pearl. What then is preferable, the pearl or the healthy oyster? Cue for more dialectics.

Notes to Chapter 6

1. The major exceptions are *Kleines Organon für das Theater (A Short Organum for the Theatre*, 1948) and *Die Tage der Commune (The Days of the Commune*, 1948–49).
2. Bertolt Brecht, *Schriften zum Theater*, Vol. VIII, Aufbauverlag Berlin, 1964, p. 76.
3. Cf.: 'It is impossible to complete a play without a stage. . . . The stage alone decides on the possible variants.' *Der gute Mensch von Sezuan (Materialien)*, Aufbauverlag, Berlin, 1969, p. 13.
4. V. Hans-Joachim Bunge, *Antigonemodell 1948 von Bertolt Brecht und Caspar Neher*, phil. Diss. Greifswald, 1957.
5. *Stücke* XI, Suhrkamp, Frankfurt am Main, 1959, p. 100.
6. Ibid., p. 99.
7. It was no doubt for this reason, as much as for fear of embarrassing the authorities who had just set up units of the armed People's Police (*Kasernierte Volkspolizei*) that the Prologue with its pacifistic tendencies was suppressed for the East German premiere in Greiz in 1951.
8. *Stücke* XI, p. 100.
9. *Deutsche Dramaturgie der Sechziger Jahre*, ed. Gotthart Wunberg, Max Niemeyer, Tübingen, 1974, p. 141.
10. *Schriften zum Theater* VI, p. 249.
11. *Schriften zum Theater* VII, p. 58.
12. Manfred Wekwerth, *Notate. Zur Arbeit des Berliner Ensembles 1956–1966*, Aufbauverlag, Berlin, 1967, p. 121.
13. Brecht, *Arbeitsbuch*, 20 May 1951.
14. *Notate*, p. 124.
15. Ibid., p. 136.
16. *The Empty Space*, Penguin Books, Harmondsworth, 1972, p. 91, (originally published by MacGibbon & Kee).
17. *Notate*, p. 129.
18. Ibid., p. 153.
19. Ibid., p. 155.
20. *Stücke* X, Suhrkamp, Frankfurt am Main, 1957, p. 367.
21. Ibid., p. 375.
22. *Notate*, p. 100.
23. Ibid., p. 102.
24. Peter Hacks, *Ausgewählte Dramen*, Aufbauverlag, Berlin, 1972, p. 247.
25. Ibid., p. 275.

26. Ibid., p. 68.
27. Ibid., p. 147.
28. *Stücke*, Reclam, Leipzig, 1974, p. 246.
29. *Ausgewählte Dramen*, p. 339.
30. Ibid., p. 289.
31. Ibid., p. 329.
32. Ibid., p. 350.
33. Ibid., pp. 356–7.
34. Ibid., p. 123.
35. Ibid., p. 415.
36. Note of 10 January 1952, cit. Wekwerth, *Notate*, p. 61.
37. *Ausgewählte Dramen*, p. 146.
38. Ibid., p. 279.
39. Ibid., p. 125.
40. Ibid., p. 123.
41. *Stücke* V, Suhrkamp, Frankfurt am Main, 1957, p. 56.
42. Interestingly Hacks has translated Synge's *The Playboy of the Western World*.
43. Heiner Müller should not be confused with a minor East German poet and playwright, Armin Müller (b. 1928), nor with Harald Mueller (b. 1934), *Dramaturg* at the Schiller-Theater West Berlin, whose *Der grosse Wolf* (*Big Wolf*, premiere 1968 Kammerspiele Munich), a savage little play about gangs of orphans in Vietnam, has been seen at the Royal Court Theatre London under the direction of William Gaskill.
44. *Theater heute*, August 1965, p. 63.
45. *Die neuen Leiden des jungen W*, Henschelverlag, Berlin, 1974, p. 120.
46. Hans Daiber, *Theater: eine Bilanz*, Langen-Müller, Munich, 1965, p. 54.

7 Political Theatre in the West

Repeatedly, West Germany has tried to seal itself off from theatrical influences from the East. There have been three attempts to boycott Brecht's plays: after the Workers' Uprising in East Germany in 1953, after the Hungarian Revolution in 1956 and after the erection of the Berlin Wall in 1961. Harry Buckwitz, in his bold decision to perform Brecht, was obliged to defend the plays on aesthetic grounds and even then did not escape censure and public demonstrations outside his theatre. Despite this, Brecht has now become the most popular playwright on the West German stage and his influence on the flourishing political drama of the West is unmistakeable.

One of his leading directors, Peter Palitzsch, crossed to the West in 1960 and has since done important work in Frankfurt and Stuttgart. Five years later he was followed by one of East Germany's most promising dramatists, Hartmut Lange. Born in 1937, Lange worked for three years (1961–64) as *Dramaturg* at the Deutsches Theater in East Berlin. The plays he wrote from 1960 onwards did not meet with official approval, a situation he refers to without embitterment: 'Poetry is a profession which is very seldom needed'.[1] But it led to his decision to find an escape-route to the West by way of Yugoslavia. While his plays have therefore only met with recognition in the West, his writing bears all the imprints of the dialectical materialist. Indeed his *Marski* (1962–63, premiere 1966 Städtische Bühnen, Frankfurt) is strongly reminiscent of Hacks' *Moritz Tassow*. In both we have the poetic treatment of contemporary East Germany, Lange also using blank-verse passages to portray an unreal peasant society. There is too the same improbably Utopian outcome: Marski having alienated his fellow-peasants by his meanness finds himself alone and miserable. He decides to hang himself but is saved by the members of the collective. In a feast which celebrates the glorious plenty which collective-farming has achieved, Marski agrees to become one of their number. Written at a time when the radical upheaval of land reform had led to a scarcity of many food-stuffs, the play is bursting with thinly-disguised irony.

In his style there are also elements of Hacks' consciously naive approach to characterisation and dialogue. But whereas Hacks' plays have the lightness of the fairy-tale, most of Lange's are more reminiscent of a Christmas pantomime. There are the same visual tricks, grotesque figures, rough humour and robust relationship with the audience.

This is clearly seen in his savage plays attacking Stalin, who both as a historical figure and as a political concept seems to exert an obsessive fascination on Lange. Lange blames the rigidity and brutality of Stalinism for the failure of a truly communist revolution, just as he appears to blame Trotsky for his failure to rid the world of Stalin when he had the opportunity (in *Trotzki in Coyoacan*, 1972, premiere 1972 Deutsches Schauspielhaus, Hamburg).

His two major anti-Stalinist plays are *Hundsprozess* and *Herakles* (*Dog's Trial* and *Heracles* 1964–67, premiere 1968 Schaubühne am Halleschen Ufer, Berlin). The first of these is a nightmarish vision of a Stalinist show-trial, in the course of which the friends of the defendant are decapitated and provided with dogs' heads so that, Animal-Farm-style, they can bark in obedient chorus. The second shows Stalin as Heracles, trying to put the world to rights but only making matters worse because of his uncontrolled brutality.

His most sophisticated and successful play to date has been the comedy *Die Gräfin von Rathenow* (*The Countess of Rathenow* 1969, premiere 1969 Bühnen der Stadt, Cologne). Based on Kleist's *novelle*, *Die Marquise von O.*, it tells how a Prussian Countess discovers she is pregnant without having any idea who the father might be. The father is in fact a French lieutenant who had saved the swooning Countess from a burning building and had violated her before she regained consciousness. Falling in love with her, the Lieutenant passionately woos her in the hope of marrying her before she bears the child. But Prussian honour will not allow such easy solutions: the father must be found. When it turns out to be the Lieutenant himself, the Countess' father satisfies offended honour by shooting his future son-in-law, arranging a hurried wedding with the wounded bridegroom, and seeing to it that bride and groom go their different ways. While the first version of the play still held out some hope of a future reconciliation, the 1962 version (premiere Thalia-Theater, Hamburg) ends with the Lieutenant shooting himself as he boards his carriage. The Countess resolutely drives off. In the *Aneignung* of Kleist's story Lange has shown the lightness and warmth of the French temperament contrasted with the harsh and unbending sense of honour of the Prussians. Just as his sympathies clearly lie with weak but humane Trotsky, so he obviously prefers the life-affirming, irresponsible Frenchman. But he cannot avoid the unnerving recognition that it is Stalin and the Prussians who win the victories.

When one looks from the East to the beginnings of political drama in the West, it is as though one had stepped from the London School of Economics into a club in St. James'. Slowly shaking off the compulsion to come to terms with the Nazi past, the first political plays of the sixties were imprecise, unanalytical and couched in the language of nineteenth century ethics. A typical example was the very successful play by the novelist Siegfried Lenz (b. 1926), *Zeit der Schuldlosen* (*Time of the Guiltless* 1960–61, premiere 1961 Deutsches Schauspielhaus, Hamburg). It established a record for its day by being performed as many as forty times in one season, the sort of run that would be accounted a 'flop' in the West End of London! It falls neatly into two halves: in the first a number of citizens, named only according to their occupations, find themselves imprisoned with a political prisoner who has attempted to assassinate the Governor. The citizens will not be released until they have extracted the names of the assassin's accomplices or have persuaded him to change his allegiance to the Governor. When all their entreaties have proved fruitless and there seems to be no hope of their regaining freedom, one of their number murders the assassin by night and they are all released. The second half takes place four years later. There has been a revolution, the Governor has been overthrown and the same group has been brought together again to establish the identity of the murderer. After accusations and counter-accusations, the admission has to be made that all of them desired the death of the prisoner, had 'carried it out in their minds' and so all are guilty: 'Neglecting to act does not mean freedom from guilt. No-one becomes pure by refusing to participate'.[2] The cynical but humane Baron finally takes upon himself the guilt of them all by suddenly committing suicide.

It is significant that it is the aristocrat who makes the final grand gesture, for the emphasis is not on political insight but on heroic self-sacrifice as a means of lessening the guilt we all are heir to. Nowhere is any consideration given to the question whether the post-revolutionary order is better or worse than the Governor's rule. Instead, words like dignity, conviction, sacrifice and conscience abound. Commitment, it seems, is what is needed, without too much concern about the idea to which one is committed.

Against this background of theatrically unadventurous pseudo-political Western drama the finest political play since Brecht exploded like a bombshell. I am referring to *Die Verfolgung und Ermordung Jean Paul Marats dargestellt durch die Schauspielgruppe des Hospizes zu Charenton unter Anleitung des Herrn de Sade* (*The Persecution and Assassination of Marat as Performed by the Inmates of the Asylum of Charenton under the Direction of the Marquis de Sade* 1962–64, premiere 1964 Schiller Theater, Berlin). This was not the first play by Peter Weiss (b. 1916) painter, novelist and playwright, who has lived in Sweden since 1939. It was the play, however, which shot him from obscurity into international fame, with immediate requests by Peter Brook in London, Roger Planchon in Paris and Ingmar Bergman in Stockholm to direct it in their own theatres.

The *Marat/Sade* was a landmark in Weiss' own development as well as in the European theatre as a whole. For Weiss it represented the abandonment of the dream-like symbolism of his early plays: *Der Turm* (*The Tower* 1948, premiere 1949 Studio Stockholm, German-language premiere 1967 Theater am Belvedere, Vienna); *Die Versicherung* (*The Insurance* 1952, premiere 1966 University of Göteborg, German language premiere 1969 Bühnen der Stadt, Cologne); and *Nacht mit Gästen* (*Night with Guests* 1962–63, premiere 1962 Schiller Theater Werkstatt, Berlin).

These all suffered from obscurity and heavy-handedness, written during a period when Weiss was strongly under the acknowledged influence of Strindberg and Kafka. Significantly, it was when he began to learn from Brecht that the basis of a political drama was formed:

> Brecht influenced me as a dramatist. I learnt most from Brecht. I
> learnt clarity from him, the necessity of making clear the social

question in a play. I learnt from his lightness. He is never heavy in the psychological German way.[3]

Marat/Sade is important if for no other reason than that it holds the nightmare visions of Weiss' early plays in balance with the political debates of his later work. In more general terms it combines the emotional shocks of Artaud with the social relevance of Brecht.

Weiss has been repeatedly attracted to the figure of the outsider (Trotsky, Hölderlin, the Jews) and had already planned a radio-play about the nightmarish visions of the French Revolutionary Marat, as he sat suffering in his bath-tub. Marat was forced into this humiliating situation by the almost unbearable skin-disease he had contracted while hiding from his political enemies in the sewers, and it was in his bath that he was stabbed to death by the young fanatical Girondist, Charlotte Corday.

Then Weiss made two important discoveries: first, it was the Marquis de Sade who had held Marat's funeral oration, and secondly, while Sade was incarcerated in the Asylum of Charenton he had written plays and directed the inmates in them. These facts provided the inspiration for the confrontation between Sade and Marat in a lunatic asylum setting.

There are three levels of action. The central 'story' is minimal: as in history, Corday comes three times to Marat's door and murders him. The place is Marat's house, the time 1793. The framework action is provided by the asylum inmates under the direction of Sade with the audience being invited to identify with a contemporary Napoleonic audience. The place is Charenton, the time 1808. In addition, there are the unmistakable references to the situation of a modern audience with the ironic assurances by the Herald and the Asylum Director that all this is of the past. In this sense the place is the theatre, the time the present. Three levels of action, three levels of reality.

In performance this richness of texture creates great problems. Each actor has to cope with three levels by representing a lunatic acting a role. He and the director must decide how naturalistically the patients are to behave. Where the decision is taken to create the illusion of real mental illness, as in Peter Brook's brilliant production, there is the danger that the fascination of the setting with its attendant emotional shocks will obscure the central debate of the play. Where the setting itself is stylised, the sense of a play-within-a-play is considerably weakened, as in the Swinarski premiere in Berlin. The choice is between Artaud and Brecht, for Weiss' play, it must be admitted, is a juxtaposition rather than a synthesis of the two styles.

On the other hand, it is these very complexities that lend *Marat/Sade* much of its theatrical power. Because it is lunatics who are performing the play, there are opportunities for a naive, rough theatre, reminiscent of the circus and the fair-ground, an idiom which Weiss was to exploit in his later political revues. Furthermore, as Weiss remarked: 'In such an environment you can say virtually anything. Amongst lunatics you've got complete freedom. You can say very dangerous and crazy things, anything at all, and at the same time introduce the political agitation for which you're trying to get a hearing.'[4] On the imagined audience of 1808 as on the actual one of 1964 one of the oldest pieces of dialectic is being employed: the wisdom of the fool. Primarily, though, the asylum setting illumines the central debate between Sade and Marat. It stands as a metaphor for the society of Revolutionary France; on the one hand it reflects the continuing oppression in the tyrannous regime of the clinic, on the other it constantly undermines the political arguments of Marat by showing his listeners to be uncontrolled and resistant to change.

But then it is Sade who has supposedly written the play, so it is predictable that he will come out better in the debate with Marat. Marat stands for violent and radical social revolution. Sade is the cynic who believes only in himself. Marat wishes to improve man's situation through social change; his enemies are the reactionaries. Sade believes the only way to greater awareness is for the individual to explore himself, his enemy is the 'unbreakable iceberg-face' of Nature, the hideous fact of man's unending cruelty to man, beside which political talk seems like the ravings of a lunatic.

With characteristic cynicism Sade has distributed the roles of his play to accord with his view of political activity: Marat is played by a paranoiac, Corday by a narcoleptic, the Girondist deputy Duperret by an erotomaniac. Despite the protests of the ineffectual Asylum Director Coulmier, Sade stages scenes of violence and hysteria, until at the very end the patients run riot and Sade laughs triumphantly. Seen in this light, revolution can never succeed, because even the most radical upheaval leaves untouched the real source of man's suffering: the nature of Man himself. So the optimism of 1789 leads to the Reign of Terror which leads to the dictatorship of Napoleon. Myth wins out against History.

But does it? For after all, why does Sade write his play? Why does he trouble to provide Marat with so many powerful lines, if he believes none of it? The answer must be that in this play Sade (and behind him Weiss) is rehearsing the arguments for and against real political involvement. It seems that Sade wants to quieten the naggings of his political conscience by constantly affirming his disillusionment, but ultimately he fails. The thirty-three scenes of the play hardly seem to form any sort of progression, until one recognises that Sade is attempting to seduce Marat (his political persona) from the course of revolution. Initially, Sade's attempts are misguided: the pleas of the homely Simonne for Marat to spare himself, the visions of horror in Corday's monologues, the re-enactment of the Reign of Terror (which in fact postdated Marat's death) and above all the narration of the bloody execution of Damiens, all these are brushed aside by Marat. Unconcerned about his personal suffering, well used to violence and horror, he rises confidently above these 'sadistic' methods and repeatedly insists on issuing his fourteenth of July call to the people of France. Sade has only slightly more success with his critique of revolution as an impersonal and mechanistic force (in Scene 22 after the whipping Marat feels plunged into darkness) and again with the invocation of nightmarish figures from Marat's past (Scene 26). The turning-point comes in the second half of the play when Sade demands to know what is to become of Marat's revolution:

But Marat how will you fare in the new rearranged
   France you yearn for

Do you want someone to rule you
to control the words you write
and tell you
what work you must do
and repeat to you the new laws
over and over
until you can recite them in your sleep[5]

With this, the ultimate challenge to revolutionary thought and action,
the reminder that historically all revolutions have had to defend
themselves with the same repressiveness against which they were
fought, Marat sinks into doubt:

Why is everything so confused now
Everything I wrote or spoke
was considered and true
each argument was sound
And now
doubt
Why does everything sound false[6]

Sade appears to have won. The moment is ripe for the murder to put the
seal on Marat's defeat, and the preparations are made. But Marat comes bouncing back with 'No/I am right/and I will say it once more,'[7] for
the fifth time announcing his call to the nation. Sade uses the final
weapon in his armoury: he presents Corday, 'an untouched virgin', as a
sexual offering to Marat. He tries to deflect Marat from his idealism by
offering him the real experience of physical satisfaction. He even gets
the patients to mime copulation (since so much of the action is intended
to be played out for Marat's benefit, he should be placed behind it up-
stage instead of in the downstage position indicated by the stage-
directions). At the very moment of his murder, however, Marat is
beginning to dictate his call to the People of France and he dies with pen
and paper in his hands. Sade may have 'won' (it could hardly be
otherwise), but it is an empty victory. The political conscience has not
been silenced.

This reading of the play shows not only that it is much better constructed than is generally recognised but also that it is an extremely
relevant document of the sixties. For Sade's interior debate is not only
that of Peter Weiss but also, I believe it fair to say, of most of today's
audiences. Like Peter Weiss, few of us are complacent about the world
in which we live: the Director of the Asylum, the smug bourgeois, is
deservedly given short shrift in the play. Given then that there must be
change, is the change to be social or individual, is the revolution without
or within? Most of us in the West find it hard to commit ourselves to
either Marat's socialism or Sade's solipsism. As Weiss confessed:

It would be much better if I could say of myself: 'I'm a convinced
Communist' or 'I'm an extreme Socialist.' Then I could say
something. But I stand in the middle. I represent the third viewpoint, which I don't like myself. Perhaps if I continue writing, I can
gradually work through to an overall conception. I write to find
out where I stand, and so each time I have to bring in all my
doubts. Up till now I see no alternative, but I hope to discover it
one day.[8]

69

That day came sooner than he expected. A year later, in 1965, he had been converted to radical socialism and rejected the position he had defined in the interview quoted above. He strongly approved of Hanns Anselm Perten's production of *Marat/Sade* in Rostock, East Germany, in which Marat was made a much stronger figure than in Western productions and Sade appeared as a decadent aristocrat devoid of a valid viewpoint. Weiss also revised the text of his play, removing for example the reference to Marat's paranoia and the sentence in the Postscript which warned that Marat's ideas 'come perilously near to the idea of dictatorship.'[9]

After the fullness and excitement of *Marat/Sade*, Weiss' subsequent plays come as something of a disappointment. In the first flush of conversion his political drama has lost its sense of dialectic and preaches the Socialist message with evangelical fervour. We shall return to these pieces in the next chapter on Documentary Drama.

His most recent play, however,—apart from a dramatisation of Kafka's *Der Prozess* (*The Trial*, premiere 1975 Bremen)—is a more obvious successor to *Marat/Sade*. For in *Hölderlin* (1970–71, premiere 1971 Staatstheater, Stuttgart) Weiss is again drawn to the themes of insanity and revolution. *Hölderlin* was a Swabian poet writing at the time of Goethe and Schiller who spent the last thirty-seven years of his life in madness. His mystical visions of a new age of Greek serenity about to dawn in Germany have been frequently 'misappropriated' for Nationalistic purposes, not least by the Nazis. Peter Weiss now wishes to win him for the Socialist camp. From Pierre Bertaux' critical study, *Hölderlin et la Révolution Française* (1969) Weiss learnt of Hölderlin's commitment to the idea of revolution. On this tenuous basis, Weiss transforms the poet into a forerunner of Marxism, who has to suffer not only at the hands of repressive authority and capitalism, but also before the conformist writers and thinkers of his day (Goethe, Schiller, Fichte, Hegel). Distraught and disillusioned, he withdraws into madness. At the very end of his life he is shown being visited by the 25-year-old Karl Marx, the first person to understand the outsider Hölderlin:

> That you
> half a century ago
> did not describe
> the revolution
> as a necessity
> founded on science
> but as a mythological presentiment
> is not your fault[10]

That much of the play is a distortion of historical fact is not of great importance: this is the prerogative of the historical dramatist. What is more serious is that this distortion over-simplifies the issues presented in the play. All the poet's contemporaries, unless they are revolutionaries or simple working-folk, are caricatured. It is no doubt a delight for a German audience to see their national heroes, Goethe, Schiller, Hegel and company, reduced to opportunistic Establishment figures, but it is hardly a sound basis for a dramatic conflict. The debate of *Marat/Sade* is replaced by polemic.

In the same way, the awareness of Marat's suffering is here replaced by pathos. For in *Marat/Sade* the lunatic asylum setting undercuts the heroism of Marat and by alienation makes it more real. In *Hölderlin* we have similar distancing devices: a singer to introduce scenes and comment on them, archaic language with eighteenth-century orthography and Weiss' characteristic unpunctuated free verse with occasional use of rhyming couplets. But in *Marat/Sade* the idiom of a play-within-a-play was firmly established, while here the characters have no immediate justification for their lack of reality. Insubstantial as they are, it is difficult to discover any involvement with them. Unchallenged as the political argument is, it is hard to find any involvement here either. The reaction to the play's statement can be reduced to: 'I had never seen Hölderlin in that light before', but since he has been dead for a century and a quarter, that insight is not of great topical significance.

What *Hölderlin* does have in its favour is the imaginative use of the stage. Continuing the colourful and vigorous style of his political revues, the eight stations of the play present a constant mobility of theatrical effect: amidst the political debate there are moments of violence (a young revolutionary being beaten while he sings the *Marseillaise*), moments of eroticism (the governess baring her breast in a cynical attempt to seduce Hölderlin) and moments of horror (Hölderlin, bound and strait-jacketed, being examined in the clinic, wearing a hideous mask to prevent him tearing open his face). Moments which are delightfully easy to parody but which are never gratuitous and which show that Weiss' inventiveness as a dramatist is still very much alive.

Although he too is a committed Socialist, the novelist and sculptor Günter Grass (b. 1927) is of a much more liberal hue than Peter Weiss. It is hardly thinkable, for instance, that Peter Weiss could give active support to the SPD as Grass has done. Grass has experimented with various forms of theatre, including Absurdist Drama, e.g. *Onkel, Onkel* (*Mister, Mister* premiere 1958 Bühnen der Stadt, Cologne), *Die bösen Köche* (*The Wicked Cooks*, premiere 1961 Schiller-Theater Werkstatt, Berlin). But his most important play and his major contribution to Political Drama is *Die Plebejer proben den Aufstand* (*The Plebeians Rehearse the Uprising*, 1965, premiere 1966 Schiller-Theater Berlin).

The play is set in the Berliner Ensemble on the 17th June, 1953, the day when all over East Germany there were uprisings by discontented workers protesting against excessive demands for higher productivity. Brecht is just rehearsing the Plebeians' uprising against Coriolanus when a group of workers burst in to ask him to lend his voice in support of the uprising. He refuses to commit himself to their cause, but equally rejects a request from the authorities to denounce the uprising. For while he recognises the senselessness of the workers' revolt, which is an outburst of frustration and not a coherent political action, he still cannot find it in himself to side with the rulers against them.

Instead, he withdraws into aesthetic isolation, continuing his rehearsal, involving the workers in it, recording their voices on tape, storing up observations for use on stage. Unhappy himself about being so ineffectual, Brecht appears as representing the uncomfortable 'third viewpoint'. The play ends on a paradox, as Brecht addresses the absent workers:

> You're ignorant! Guilty myself, I accuse you.
> *He exits slowly*[11]

Despite the potential interest of the situation, the play is marred by its curiously poetic treatment of the workers' uprising. The style is elevated and abounds in ellipses in a manner reminiscent of Expressionism. It is also highly improbable that workers whose fellows are rioting on the streets would be so easily induced to participate in rehearsals. Perhaps this is the point: that the play Grass is writing is *meant* to be as unrelated to reality as Brecht's work on *Coriolanus* was to the uprising outside the theatre. In which case this drama of politics is exposed as an absurdist piece whose statement is that there is nothing to state. As the *Dramaturg* Erwin says, having just saved Brecht and himself from hanging by recourse to Menenius' parable of the belly:

> Nonsense has a tradition here
> and keeps things fresh, as formalin does corpses.
> That is why progress cannot do without it.[12]

Tankred Dorst (b. 1925) has also written a number of absurdist plays, e.g. *Freiheit für Clemens* (*Freedom for Clemens* 1960, premiere 1960 Bielefeld) but in his later writing he has shown himself—after Weiss—to be the finest political dramatist in the West. His most successful play, *Toller* (1968, premiere 1968 Staatstheater, Stuttgart) has some affinities with Weiss, in particular the revue techniques: simultaneous action on different levels of the stage, puppets, songs, crowd-scenes, a cabaret act, readings from Toller's memoirs and even a scene in a lunatic asylum. Where Dorst excels over Weiss is in his characterisation. While the characters in Weiss' plays are primarily representatives of different philosophical and political viewpoints, Dorst's Toller comes to life as rounded being. The Expressionist actor/writer is portrayed in his private relationships as well as in his public difficulties as figurehead of the revolution. As in Brecht's *Die Tage der Commune*, we see here the failure of a premature attempt to establish workers' rule in the Munich Räterepublik of 1919. Again the failure is due to the political inexperience of the 'Councillors' and their hesitancy to use force to defend themselves. As the Communist leader Leviné says to Toller: 'You really must decide to think politically'.[13] But it seems that Toller is unwilling to loosen his hold on his own idealism, for he recognises the difficulty of reconciling politics with true revolution: 'Perhaps there is only a single moment when we are free—when the old order is destroyed and a new one has not yet been established. Just this one moment—and we idiots are desperately working to extend it for a century.'[14]

The final irony comes when, after the defeat of the revolution, Toller is on trial for treason. In an impassioned speech, he recognises that the course of events cannot be dictated by 'good intentions' and declares his solidarity with the violent elements of the revolution. In reply comes a shout from the gallery: 'Actor!' And despite his demands that the court should not treat him as a misguided bourgeois, he is sentenced to five years imprisonment, while the workers are led off to their execution. Not only did he fail to give a proper lead to the revolution; he is also refused the possibility of sharing in its martyrdom. Once more the ineffectuality of the bourgeois artist is observed as he stands paralysed between his liberal sense of humanity and the recognition of the need for violent change.

Dorst returns to the figure of the writer in *Eiszeit* (*Ice-Age* 1972, premiere 1973 Schauspielhaus Bochum, directed by Zadek). This time the writer is the Norwegian, Knut Hamsun, who in the last year of his life was called to account for his support of the Nazis. Although the plot is invented, the style gives the impression of depicting real events. Within this realism, however, Dorst still achieves some variety in the use of the stage: the visual humour of the aged inmates of the old people's home hanging up bunting, the abstract tests of the psychiatrist, the concert for the old people.

Here again the central character is well developed. As the Old Man (Hamsun) says of modern playwrights:

> They think they are putting a character on stage when they get a figure to express a few ideas. And then they insist: that's how he is! But a man is a conglomeration of many ideas and wishes and hopes. They are all different, contradicting one another and struggling for supremacy.[15]

Part of the complexity of the Old Man's portrayal lies in the fact that, despite his sympathies for Quisling and the Nazis, he is gentle, humane and generally likeable. It is not Dorst's purpose, however, to repeat Zuckmayer's attempt in *Des Teufels General* to show that Nazi supporters were not all bad. Rather, he continues the line established by Walser in *Eiche und Angora* by analysing post-war society in its relationship to Fascism. Of course the Old Man was wrong, he freely admits it, but then he was misled by clever propaganda. But what has contemporary society to offer that makes it so smug about its conquest of Fascism? It is left to the Old Man himself to remind his interrogators that the papers of today 'always tell the truth'. This questionable assertion of the truthfulness of the media is the only positive quality that is evident in the new order that presumes to accuse the Old Man. For the rest it seems motivated by a negative and self-righteous desire for revenge. The sterility of our civilisation does indeed seem a new ice-age, adding point to the Old Man's question about post-war youth: 'Do they also have great and beautiful ideas? New ideas, which none of us has yet thought of?'[16]

In this unanswered question there is reflected again the dilemma of the modern writer, the dilemma shared by Weiss until 1965, by Grass' Brecht-figure, by Dorst's Toller. Profoundly dissatisfied with the society in which he lives, he nevertheless cannot commit himself fully to a Communist ideology, however politically successful, because it has failed as yet to fulfil the promise of Socialist revolution.

So long as the writer remains unaffected by the realities of Communist rule, he can champion this alternative to capitalism from a standpoint of comparative assurance (cf. Brecht up to 1949, Peter Hacks up to 1955). But the writers of East Germany, like Hacks and Müller, who have tried to analyse the shortcomings of their society have met with repeated difficulties and have until recently been forced to withdraw into the adaptation of myth and historical legend. The Western writer, witnessing this curtailment of artistic expression, seeing the repeated triumph of expediency over humanity in Eastern

Europe—whatever attempts to justify it in terms of 'defending the Revolution'—cannot lend his support to this alternative philosophy. Where there is immediate commitment, as in Hartmut Lange or Weiss after 1965, it tends to expend itself in aggression—against Stalinism and imperialism respectively. Polemic replaces dialectic.

For the rest, political commitment is to an ideal which seems to have found no home in reality and perhaps can never do so. The playwright, eager to affect the real world, all too often finds himself conjuring up visions beyond reality, asking questions that cannot be answered and demanding circumstances that cannot be achieved.

It is, I believe, from the ideological uncertainty of the Western writer, from the uncomfortable recognition of the gulf between his aesthetically shaped ideals and the actual nature of the world that Documentary Theatre was born. Here, in the supposedly objective realm of fact the playwright need no longer fear the interference of his own subjectivity.

Notes to Chapter 7

1. Hartmut Lange, *Theaterstücke 1960–72*, Rowohlt, Reinbek bei Hamburg, 1973, p. 9.
2. Siegfried Lenz, *Zeit der Schuldlosen*, Hans Bredow, Hamburg, 1961, p. 47.
3. *'Playwright of Many Interests'*, *The Times*, 19 August 1964.
4. *Materialien zu Peter Weiss' Marat/Sade*, Suhrkamp, Frankfurt/Main, 1967, p. 98.
5. Peter Weiss, *The Persecution and Assassination of Marat as Performed by the Inmates of the Asylum of Charenton under the Direction of the Marquis de Sade*, translated by Geoffrey Skelton and Adrian Mitchell, Calder & Boyars, London, 5th edition, 1970, p. 90. The first line of this quotation is an addition by the translators, but it serves to clarify the sense of the passage.
6. Ibid., p. 90.
7. Ibid., p. 96.
8. *Materialien zu Marat/Sade*, p. 99.
9. *Marat/Sade*, p. 99.
10. Peter Weiss, *Hölderlin*, Suhrkamp, Frankfurt/Main, 1971, p. 192.
11. Günter Grass, *Theaterspiele*, Luchterhand, Neuwied, 1970, p. 321.
12. Ibid., p. 295.
13. Tankred Dorst, *Toller*, Suhrkamp, Frankfurt/Main, 1968, p. 69.
14. Ibid., p. 23.
15. Tankred Dorst, *Eiszeit*, Suhrkamp, Frankfurt/Main, 1973, p. 26.
16. Ibid., p. 21.

8 The Theatre of Fact – Documentary Drama

In the early sixties Western playwrights were not only prey to ideological uncertainties; they were also unsure about their aesthetic purpose, questioning whether their subjective vision actually reflected and influenced reality. As Keith Bullivant writes:

> What was being challenged as regards the creative imagination was the authenticity of its results. Documentary literature substituted the authenticity of the material.[1]

To these general concerns was added the more immediate influence of the mass media, especially with the reportage of the Eichmann trial in 1961. The resultant surge of interest in Documentary Drama became the most important development in German theatre since the war. Moreover, for the first time since Brecht a new influence on world theatre had its major source in Germany.

Indeed, if an English theatre-goer were asked to name a living West German playwright (which of course excludes Dürrenmatt, Frisch, Handke and—strictly—Weiss), then he would probably think of Hochhuth, the first of the documentary playwrights of the sixties. While this international fame is no guarantee of his skill as a writer, it nevertheless is proof that the theatre is still capable of stirring public controversy.

Rolf Hochhuth (b. 1931) worked for many years as a reader with a publishing firm, no doubt good training for the thorough research many of his plays have demanded. His first and still his best-known play was *Der Stellvretreter* (British title: *The Representative*, American title: *The Deputy*, 1959–62, premiere 1963 Freie Volksbühne West Berlin). It was with this play that Piscator, himself a great innovator of Documentary Theatre in the twenties, opened the new building of the Freie Volksbühne and immediately unleashed an international public discussion, the like of which had not been stimulated by any play in the history of the German theatre.

The cause of controversy, as with his other great success *Soldaten* (*Soldiers*, premiere 1967 Freie Volksbühne West Berlin) lay in Hochhuth's skill in assembling accusations against two sensitive targets, Pope Pius XII and Churchill. In *Der Stellvretreter* the case for the prosecution rests on the Pope's unwillingness to intervene on behalf of the Jews, although their arrest, deportation and extermination by the Nazis must have been known to him. Attempting to awaken the conscience of the Pope are the Jesuit priest Father Riccardo (an invented figure) and the mysterious SS officer Gerstein. But the Pope is too concerned with the suppression of 'Bolshevism' and above all the finances of the Church to risk disturbing the Concordat between the Vatican and Hitler. In the middle of dictating a thoroughly innocuous statement containing the obliquest of references to the Jews, he interrupts himself to recommend his financial adviser to sell shares in the Hungarian railways. Disgusted by this lack of integrity, the young priest Riccardo resolves to accompany a transport of Jews to Auschwitz and to their death. As he had declared earlier:

> And since the Pope, though only a man,
> can even represent *God* on earth,
> then I'll ... then a poor priest if need be
> can also represent the Pope—*there*
> where he should be standing today.[2]

Through his martyrdom Riccardo becomes the true 'representative'.

Piscator begins his Preface to the published version of the play with the words: 'Hochhuth's play *The Representative* is one of the few really significant attempts to come to terms with the past.'[3] He praises it on two grounds: first, because it maintains the tradition of Schillerian historical drama in insisting on the freedom of each individual to take moral decisions; secondly, because it rises above private situations to 'an objective examination of the totality of human behaviour, history not a story.'[4] Unfortunately these two elements are hardly compatible, and the play suffers from its lack of clarity on the issue of individual responsibility. On the one hand, Hochhuth suggests that different roles should be played by the same actor, because 'in the age of general conscription it is not necessarily a question of merit or blame, or even a question of character, whether a man wears this or that uniform or is on the side of the hangman or victim.'[5] On the other hand, there is moral condemnation of those who do not choose to oppose the hangman and side with the victim. Added to this confusion on the moral issue, there is also a tendency in Hochhuth to lift events onto a superhuman level. Thus much of the action of the play may be seen as a conflict between the good angel Gerstein and the devilish Doctor who 'welcomes' the victims at Auschwitz. Gerstein is described as being 'so "modern" a Christian that in order to understand him fully it is necessary to read Kierkegaard'.[6] Such erudition is not required to recognise the old-world character of the Doctor: 'He incorporates absolute evil (Er hat das Format des absolut Bösen) . . . an ancient figure of the theatre and of Christian mystery-plays.'[7] Significantly enough, both these figures mysteriously disappeared after the war, Gerstein in a Paris prison, the Doctor, Hochhuth suggests, in the direction of South America. By introducing this idea that the forces of good and evil are locked in struggle on a higher plane, Hochhuth further reduces the autonomy of the individual.

No-one can blame him for failing to make up his mind on the issue of free-will and determination. After all, who has—to anybody else's satisfaction? But one can take Hochhuth to task when he tries to assume the mantle of modernity by documenting the political and economic pressures which determined the behaviour of recent public figures, while at the same time clinging to traditional concepts of Schillerian free-will and metaphysical conflicts between good and evil. One may not go as far as Armand Gatti in condemning *Der Stellvertreter* as 'the worst kind of bourgeois hypocrisy', but one must agree with Werner Mittenzwei when he says:

> Hochhuth's technique does indeed allow a close relationship between political action and quite individual characterisation, but it fails whenever it is a question of causal relationships in society, of what goes on behind what goes on.[8]

Not only is there confusion in the statement of the play but also in its style. Although Hochhuth is at pains to claim an authentic atmosphere for his pieces, as a dramatist with literary pretensions he shies away from 'a documentary naturalism devoid of style in the manner of a newsreel'.[9] So where there should be banality, he seeks to give his writing 'style'; where there should be bald prose, he uses free verse which is often inappropriate to the subject. The most embarrassing example occurs at the beginning of the Fifth Act, where three Jews en route for Auschwitz are given monologues in a grand classical style. If their tragedy *can* be encompassed, then it is not by the minor talent of Hochhuth: the effect is one of melodrama and pathos.

His other major documentary drama, *Soldaten*, succeeds better in this respect, as the use of 'rhythmic prose' in the central play is less incongruous with the realistic characters and incidents. Admittedly, there is a heavily written *Rahmenspiel*, or outer play, in verse, with a number of symbolic figures and other Expressionistic devices. It is this outer play that explains the sub-title *Nekrolog auf Genf* (*Obituary of Geneva*). In it Dorland, a repentant former RAF commander, plans to stage a play in the ruins of Coventry Cathedral to mark the hundredth anniversary of the Geneva Convention. The purpose of Dorland's piece is to press for an extension of the Geneva Convention to protect civilians from bombing, but his play is banned from performance. The central action, which we are invited to regard as a rehearsal, deals with the problems faced by Churchill in 1943, in particular the decision about the bombing of German cities and the embarrassment caused by the exiled Polish leader Sikorski, who threatens to disturb the alliance between Britain and the Soviet Union. In both cases Churchill is shown to place expediency above humanity—by ordering the bombing of German civilians and by acquiescing in the assassination of Sikorski. There is no proof that Sikorski's death was anything more than an accident, as a lengthy action for libel has shown, but this is the concern of the historian. What is interesting from the dramatic aspect is that Hochhuth seems more ready to recognise the political forces to which Churchill was subject and so does not condemn him as roundly as Pope Pius XII. One of many indications is the stage-direction at the end of Act One: 'as though Churchill were free to choose'.[10]

Yet here again there is confusion between Hochhuth's recognition of the part played by economic forces in determining political decisions and his desire to introduce some noumenal element. Dorland may say:

We all like earning money—so:
if men earn money from the *war*,
it's only *human* to want war. . . .
In the theatre of war the man who gets the *takings*
is the one who sits in the *gallery*.[11]

But Hochhuth does not pursue the implications of these economic arguments, seeking instead the great movements of history in the decisions of individuals. In an attempt to develop Churchill's charisma, and incidentally abdicating his role as a writer, Hochhuth inserts the note:

This is the moment in the play where the author can achieve nothing more and the actor everything to make the *leap* that will turn comedy into myth.[12]

Although he has now stopped writing documentary plays, perhaps because the world is running short of respected figures about whom one can stir up controversy, one of Hochhuth's recent plays contains many of the elements of the earlier two. *Guerillas* (premiere 1970 Staatstheater Stuttgart) describes a bold plot to take over the United States and to establish an egalitarian society by disposing of a limited number of industrialists who hold power in their hands. Once again Hochhuth sees the relationship between capital and power, but he is naive enough to suppose that a coup by one individual senator might effect a change.

Many of Hochhuth's difficulties in writing documentary drama would seem to be inherent in the genre itself. The main justification for documentary drama, and what distinguishes it from other historical drama, is its claim to objectivity. There is of course the problem of the selection and evaluation of documents which must introduce an element of subjectivity. Moreover, in order to bring documents to life on stage, Hochhuth found it necessary to invent leading characters (Father Riccardo) and events (e.g. the meeting between Churchill and the Bishop of Chichester), so making his plays not much different from most historical drama. We have observed too that the attempt to lend 'style' to documentary material can give it a hollow ring. Finally, it has been recognised at least since Tolstoy's *War and Peace* that individuals do not create history, and yet drama has traditionally been concerned with individual cases. This difficulty, already clearly recognised by Dürrenmatt a decade before, is made evident in Hochhuth by his comprehensive notes which are inserted in the text of his plays or appended at the back. They in fact often contain the most exciting information, as when we are told in *Soldaten* that at the age of 38 Churchill was in command of the biggest armada in the history of mankind, and that 33 years later he was directing an invasion involving 5,000 ships and 11,000 aircraft.[13] The vast scale of modern warfare cannot be contained within the limits of conventional dramaturgy.

While Hochhuth failed to solve these difficulties, it was due to him and Piscator that documentary drama became established as a genre in the sixties. It was taken a stage further by Heinar Kipphardt. Born in 1922, he qualified as a doctor, practised for a while in Düsseldorf and Berlin, but in 1950 became *Dramaturg* at the Deutsches Theater in East Berlin. He crossed to the West in 1960 and was *Dramaturg* at the

Munich Kammerspiele from 1968 to 1971. Ironically, he had to leave this post because he was accused of being too left-wing.

One of his documentaries, *Joel Brand* (1964–65, premiere 1965 Kammerspiele Munich) is very much akin to Hochhuth's plays, although the style is much simpler. Like Hochhuth, Kipphardt uses documentary sources as the basis of a dramatised reconstruction. The action is again set in the Second World War and presents, as the sub-title has it, *Die Geschichte eines Geschäfts* (*The Story of a Deal*). The 'deal' is one proposed by Eichmann, that the Allies should exchange army lorries for Jews who will otherwise be sent to the gas-chambers. Joel Brand is to act as intermediary with the British authorities. Here again the promptings of humanity are seen in collision with the primary objective of ending the war. Charged with a mission of life and death, Joel Brand is repeatedly frustrated by petty bureaucracy and the obduracy of the British authorities. On the one hand, the British fear that the main objective of Eichmann's proposed 'deal' is to drive a wedge between the vital alliance of the Soviet Union with the West; on the other, they refuse to bargain with 'criminals'. Captain Tunney of the British Secret Service may be more honourable than Eichmann, but he is no less implacable: 'The British Government cannot negotiate with mass-murderers about blackmail.'[14] To governments today who face the dilemma of acceding to or resisting terrorists' demands, these words have a prophetic ring.

Kipphardt's other important documentary, also directed by Piscator, took the genre a stage further by showing its suitability for court-room drama: *In der Sache J. Robert Oppenheimer* (*In the Matter of J. Robert Oppenheimer*, premiere 1964 Freie Volksbühne West Berlin and Kammerspiele Munich). It established a record, only superseded by Dürrenmatt's *Play Strindberg*, by being taken up into the repertory of 22 different theatres in its first season—an indication of the tremendous popularity of documentary theatre.

Interestingly enough, Kipphardt insists that *Oppenheimer* is 'a literary text, not a document'.[15] Thus, like Hochhuth, he declares his interest in stylistic quality and in the need to extract general relevance from an individual situation. Kipphardt has taken the transcript of the 1954 hearings into the atomic scientist Oppenheimer's application for a security clearance, and has transformed 3,000 pages of typescript into an actable piece. By thus confining himself to one body of documentary material relating to a specific question, Kipphardt has solved many of the difficulties Hochhuth found himself in. He has discovered the con tent suitable for the form.

The theme of *Oppenheimer* is one which has preoccupied German playwrights since the war: the responsibility of the scientist in the atomic age. Curiously—but perhaps understandably—for a nation which itself possesses no atomic bombs, Germany has shown a very alert conscience on this issue. The one major philosophical work on the subject, Karl Jaspers' *Die Atombombe und die Zukunft des Menschen* (*The Atom-Bomb and the Future of Man*, 1961) has come from Germany, and ever since Galileo's cry of self-reproach: 'I have betrayed my calling',[16] the dilemma of the scientist has been repeatedly examined on the German stage, notably by Carl Zuckmayer in *Das kalte Licht* (*The Cold Light*, premiere 1955 Deutsches Schauspielhaus Hamburg),

Hans Henny Jahnn in *Der staubige Regenbogen* (*The Dusty Rainbow*, 1959, premiere 1961 Städtische Bühnen Frankfurt, directed by Piscator), Friedrich Dürrenmatt in *Die Physiker* (*The Physicists*, premiere 1962) and Ernst Schumacher in *Die Versuchung des Forschers* (*The Temptation of a Research Scientist*, premiere 1975 Volkstheater Rostock).

For Oppenheimer, the problem is especially acute, since it was he who was primarily responsible for the bomb that was dropped on Hiroshima. While he could accept the need for urgency to end the Second World War, he has subsequently dragged his heels in the pursuit of military research, fearing the loss of freedom for which the war had been fought. At the height of the McCarthy-ite investigations he must assert: 'There are people who are prepared to defend freedom until there is no more of it left.'[17] Too late he recognises the need for the scientist to take a moral stand. Science can provide man with freedom from drudgery and want; it can also destroy the whole earth. 'Standing at this cross-roads, we scientists sense that we have never had such importance and that we have never been so powerless.'[18] Oppenheimer is refused his security clearance. The authorities are quite right: a war-machine cannot use a scientist with a conscience.

The documentary reportage of a trial was used to its greatest effect by Peter Weiss in *Die Ermittlung* (*The Investigation*, 1964–65). The premiere on the 19 October 1965 was more in the nature of a requiem for the victims of Auschwitz than a purely theatrical occasion. For the first time in the history of drama, a play was premiered on the same night in 17 different theatres in both East and West. Piscator directed it for the Freie Volksbühne in West Berlin; Karl von Appen, Erich Engel, Manfred Wekwerth and others collaborated on directing an imposing cast in the Deutsche Akademie der Künste in East Berlin; and Peter Brook found time for this commercially impracticable venture by presenting it in a midnight reading with the Royal Shakespeare Company at the Aldwych.

The strength of the play lies in its extreme discipline. Where Hochhuth and Kipphardt had attempted to give 'style' to their writing, Weiss recognised that the hideous facts which came to light in the Auschwitz trials of 1962–64 in Frankfurt should be allowed to speak for themselves. As he wrote in 1968:

> Documentary theatre refrains from all invention, it takes authentic material and reproduces it on stage without altering the content but by adapting the form. ... Critical selection and the way in which extracts of reality are juxtaposed determine the quality of documentary drama.[19]

Quality is therefore no longer to be achieved by imaginative rewriting of documentary material, but by selection and presentation. In *Die Ermittlung* we have a 'distillation' ('Konzentrat') in eleven 'Cantos' of the proceedings of the Frankfurt trials which Weiss himself had attended. Everything is bared down to essentials. The language is economical, subjected to the characteristic discipline of Weiss by being printed as free verse without punctuation. There should be no attempt to recreate the court-room, and the witnesses are numbered and anonymous: they are 'mere mouthpieces, ... reporting what hundreds testified to'.[20] The most obvious authorial involvement is in the stage-directions, which now and again require the generally unrepentant and self-satisfied defendants to break into laughter. This grotesque merriment set beside the horrors described by the witnesses is one of the most disturbing features of the play.

In addition to these formal aspects, Weiss' selection of material is unashamedly tendentious. Like Walser and Dorst, he questions contemporary West German attitudes to the Nazi past. Moreover, as a Marxist, Weiss agrees with Brecht that Fascism is an extreme manifestation of capitalism, and it is against capitalist society that some of the criticism is levelled:

> Many of those who were destined
> to act as prisoner
> had grown up with the same ideas
> as those
> who ended up playing the role of guards . . .
> We must rid ourselves of the sublime view
> that we cannot understand what the camp was like
> We all knew the society
> which created the regime
> that could bring forth such camps
> We were familiar with the basis
> of the social order that was in force
> so we could also find our way
> when that order was pushed to the last extremity
> in which the exploiter might develop his power
> to an extent hitherto unknown.[21]

By going much further than Hochhuth in accepting the interchangeability of roles, Weiss in both form and content shows how social and political forces determine the guilt of the defendants. Significantly, the Counsel for the Defence, who speaks with the voice of modern Germany, dismisses the implications of this view:

> We most firmly reject
> this kind of theory
> in which a distorted ideology
> is reflected.[22]

In refusing to accept a political theory that might in fact lessen the individual responsibility of his clients, the Counsel for the Defence shows himself more concerned with the question of 'distorted ideology' than of mitigating circumstances. Whatever the outcome, the defence will not allow capitalism to be put on trial. For this reason Weiss ends his play in the spirit of Coulmier in *Marat/Sade* with an ironical plea to accept all this as belonging to the past:

> All of us
> I'd like to insist once more
> did nothing but our duty
> even if it often seemed hard
> and we felt close to despair
> Today

when our nation once again
has worked its way up
to a leading position
we ought to concern ourselves with other things
than with recriminations
which should long ago have been regarded
as finished and dealt with
Loud sounds of agreement by the Defendants[23]

After the ambiguities of Hochhuth and the open-ended nature of Kipphardt's plays, Weiss' documentary is seen to be much more overtly political. The abstract title of *Die Ermittlung* is indication of this. Replacing the individuals in the titles of earlier documentaries, we have here an 'investigation'. Moreover, it is an investigation into continuing wrongs in West Germany, whereas there is the implication in Hochhuth and Kipphardt that the Pope, Churchill, the Allies and Oppenheimer are all equally war-criminals—a convenient way of lightening the burden of German guilt. Weiss' political documentary challenges his own society. For him authenticity does not mean objectivity:

> Documentary theatre takes sides. Many of its themes can only lead to condemnation. For such a theatre objectivity is in certain circumstances a concept which serves to excuse the acts of vested interests. The demand for moderation and understanding is shown to be the demand of those who do not wish to lose their advantage.[24]

Since *Die Ermittlung*, Weiss has moved even further towards open political statement in his documentaries. In so doing he has pursued the documentary revue technique of Joan Littlewood, Peter Brook and Roger Planchon. His two major pieces are a protest about Portuguese colonialism in Angola, *Gesang vom Lusitanischen Popanz* (*Song of the Lusitanian Bogey*, 1966, world premiere 1967 Scala Teatern Stockholm, German premiere 1967 Schaubühne am Halleschen Ufer Berlin, directed by Karl Paryla), and an attack on United States involvement in Vietnam entitled *Diskurs über die Vorgeschichte und den Verlauf des lang andauernden Befreiungskrieges in Viet Nam als Beispiel für die Notwendigkeit des bewaffneten Kampfes der Unterdrückten gegen ihre Unterdrücker sowie über die Versuche der Vereinigten Staaten von Amerika die Grundlagen der Revolution zu vernichten* (*Discourse on the Background and the Course of the Long-lasting War of Liberation in Viet Nam as an Example of the Necessity of Armed Struggle by the Oppressed against Their Oppressors as well as on Attempts of the United States of America to Destroy the Bases of Revolution*, 1966–68, premiere 1968 Städtische Bühnen Frankfurt, directed by Harry Buckwitz).

The polemical nature of the content is clear enough from the title of *Vietnam-Diskurs*. For Weiss, the Portuguese presence in Angola and the United States presence in Vietnam 'can only be presented as unequivocal crimes. In the portrayal of looting and genocide a black-and-white technique is justified.'[25] Dialogue no longer has the function, as in Hochhuth, of defining individual attitudes, but is closer to the speech-balloons of the comic strip. Indeed, the style is very much that of the comic strip, as an extract from Weiss' notes on the documentary indicates:

> In the quotations the typical is emphasised. Figures are caricatured, situations drastically simplified. Reports, commentaries, summaries are given in songs. Introduction of chorus and mime. Theatrical presentation (Gestisches Ausspielen) of the action, parody, use of masks and props. Musical accompaniment. Sound-effects.[26]

This buoyant treatment of political documentary may well make for an entertaining and challenging evening in the theatre, but it can have few claims to being drama of lasting worth. So it has become the characteristic style of politically committed fringe groups like Theatermanufaktur, formerly known as Floh de Cologne. Already both *Gesang vom Lusitanischen Popanz* and *Vietnam-Diskurs* have themselves become documents, as is the case with the spate of political revues that resulted from student protests in 1967–68. The two most important of these were Michael Hatry's *Notstandsübung* (*Practising for a State of Emergency*, premiere 1968 Ulmer Hochschule für Gestaltung) and Günter Wallraff's *Nachspiele* (*Games That Followed*, premiere 1968 'as a work of commission for the First Article of the Constitution on the Dignity of Man', Ruhr Festival, Recklinghausen). Wallraff's *Nachspiele* deals not only with student protest and the shooting of Benno Ohnesorg and Rudi Dutschke, but also with the disturbing practices of the political courts of the *Verfassungsschutz* (Protection of the Constitution) and the conduct of employers in West Germany. Its particular quality lies in a documentary discipline reminiscent of *Die Ermittlung*. In contrast with Hatry who writes: 'We have to shout so that we'll be heard',[27] the note of *Nachspiele* is one of restraint. The text consists almost entirely of statements by the right-wing press and officials. As they damn themselves out of their own mouths, the effect is much more powerful than that of a left-wing diatribe.

Peter Weiss has proved his competence in the three principal modes of documentary drama: *Die Ermittlung* is the most powerful piece of the sixties based on a court-hearing; he developed the documentary revue from a cabaret act to a literary genre; and he has also written one significant historical reconstruction based on documentary material: *Trotzki im Exil* (*Trotsky in Exile*, 1968–69, premiere 1970 Schauspielhaus Düsseldorf, directed by Harry Buckwitz). The play begins with Trotsky's deportation by the Red Army in 1928 and ends with his assassination in Mexico in 1940. Thus, although there are flash-backs to Tsarist Russia and to the Revolutions of 1905 and 1917, the title is justified. Moreover, there is another sense in which Trotsky is still in exile to this day: despite de-Stalinisation, Trotsky's contribution to the Russian Revolution is still denied in the Soviet Union. Trotsky had to go into exile, because he insisted on preserving the humanity of Communism, while Stalin was prepared to take any measures against elements he feared might threaten the state. Weiss would like to see Trotsky's message more clearly heard in the Socialist countries to which he lends critical support, and he would certainly agree with Trotsky's words:

Against Socialism that other system still stands firm: the system of absolute baseness, absolute greed, absolute selfishness. That system cannot change. It can only, by its very nature, become more predatory, more destructive. But socialism, in spite of the crimes committed in its name, can change. It can be improved, can be given new life.[28]

The tone of these lines, in their rather dry theorising, is fairly typical of the piece. There is even a lengthy undramatic scene (Scene 12) in which Trotsky holds a kind of Brains Trust for the benefit of a number of international students.

The dynamic of the play is further weakened by Weiss' regard for authenticity. While Hochhuth reduced his characters to a large but manageable number, and Weiss himself used the technique of a limited number of actors assuming many different anonymous roles, here there are 62 named parts in addition to workers, soldiers, students, convicts and judges. Figures appear and disappear as they are required to say their piece, and even with Trotsky there is no real involvement. This is of course Weiss' intention. For this reason, the play may be of interest to students of Russian history or socialist theory, but it has no obvious justification for performance on stage.

Similar objections may be made to the third significant court-room documentary of recent German theatre, Hans Magnus Enzensberger's *Das Verhör von Habana* (*The Havana Hearing*, premiere 1970 Städtische Bühnen Essen). Like *Oppenheimer*, the hearings are not a trial in the normal sense; and yet a whole ideology is on trial. The 'defendants' are Cuban exiles captured after the Bay of Pigs invasion in 1961. They appear voluntarily before the television cameras to answer questions put by Castro supporters. This provides a unique opportunity for an analysis of bourgeois attitudes: 'The ruling class can only be induced to speak fully when it has been defeated as a counter-revolution'.[29]

Enzensberger, using only authentic texts, records ten interviews, ranging from the questioning of a misled worker to that of a Batista thug. Again and again the reasonableness of the revolutionary interrogators is contrasted with the inadequaacies of the captured invaders, their rationalisations, self-delusion and evasiveness. The response of a former philosophy student is typical: 'I should on no account like to draw hasty consequences. That is something I have always abhorred.'[30] As in Weiss' reference to the self-interested 'demand for moderation and understanding', it is here used as an excuse for the refusal to recognise the errors of counter-revolution.

Enzensberger's intention is not so much to document one failed counter-revolution as to reveal to his German audiences the bankruptcy of bourgeois ideology. But his piece is unsatisfactory in two respects. First, there is no politically sophisticated apologist amongst the prisoners who are represented on stage. Not one of them, for example, justifies his attempt to halt the revolution by reference to the consistently poor historical record of violent revolutions. The process of revolution is never questioned as such; all doubts seem concerned only with asking whether it had genuine popular support. Secondly, if we concede that the audience is convinced by the revolutionary argument (and after a regime like Batista's it would be hard not to be), then there is the danger that this will satisfy rather than challenge the spectator. Enzensberger writes: 'The Havana Hearings do not only proceed from a revolutionary situation, they are a revolutionary act in themselves.'[31] The danger is that the audience will enter into the spirit of the revolution, play at being guerrillas for a couple of hours and return well entertained to their middle-class apartments—a manifestation of what New Yorkers call 'radical chic'. This is anyway the risk run by political theatre in a capitalist society and it is not confined to *Das Verhör von Habana*. The particular problem of this play by a writer who has made his name as a poet and not as a playwright, is that it bases itself so closely on the actual hearings in Havana that it is difficult for a West German audience to relate its statements to a European situation. Enzensberger's excellent introduction makes the points that are implicit but well hidden in the repetitious text of the play. As a comment on his achievement one might quote Weiss again: '. . . documentary theatre that wishes primarily to be a political forum and dispenses with artistic execution throws itself into question.'[32] Enzensberger's 'document' is better suited for private study than public performance.

The most recent significant contribution to documentary drama has been Dieter Forte's *Martin Luther & Thomas Münzer oder Die Einführung der Buchhaltung* (*Martin Luther and Thomas Münzer or The Introduction of Book-keeping*, premiere 1970 Basler Theater). At first glance the 82 scenes about Luther and the Peasants' War seem like another monumental reconstruction *à la* Hochhuth, but Forte goes much deeper in his critical analysis by questioning the validity of the documents themselves. Their authenticity is not necessarily challenged, but it is shown how they will often come into being in response to political or economic pressure and therefore not truly reflect actual circumstances. In this play a fresh look is taken at Luther. Forte suggests that far from being a great reformer, he was in fact a reactionary sycophant. His famous Ninety-five Theses were not only plagiarised from a fellow academic but were published at the special request of the Elector of Saxony in order to spoil the trade in indulgences by the neighbouring Archbishop. Luther's refusal to recant at the Diet of Worms was above all a matter of economic necessity: the German princes had run themselves heavily into debt with the prospect of the Reformation dispossessing the Church lands. If Luther recanted, they were faced with bankruptcy.

The true revolutionary is Thomas Münzer, and the real power lies in the hands of Fugger, the banker and merchant. The alternative title of the play refers to the fact that the 'first great German revolution' also coincided with the introduction of book-keeping. Political power, theological discussion, social change, all these became numbers in Fugger's ledger. Money could buy votes for the Holy Roman Emperor and weapons to suppress the Peasants' Revolt.

This new view of Luther is so refreshing that it makes John Osborne's *Luther* seem as conventional as a Sunday School play. For the first time since Brecht's Galileo, a great historical figure is analysed in depth on the German stage. Moreover, Forte's style is extremely witty, using anachronisms and comic situations to maintain the interest of the audience in what might otherwise become a series of dry political incidents. Not only are weights and money updated to present values, but there are also references to an inflationary boom, to a press-conference and to a 'happening' by Leonardo da Vinci. The Emperor Maximilian's hydromania is explained away by the suggestion that he was too penniless to afford drinking anything other than water, and the Pope is an atheist whose main subject of conversation is the fashionable length for his robes. Indeed, this humorous treatment of events in a play which 'has no heroes' might run the risk of being such fun that it lost its bite. The bloody suppression of the Peasants' Revolt at the end of the play corrects this, however. The pathetic attempts by the first German Parliament to establish itself without the use of force, the mercenaries' brutality, the savage beating to death of Münzer, the executioner's demand for payment (including a fee for 'putting out the eyes and tearing out the tongues of various children'[33]); these authentic events remind the audience that the Reformation and its consequences were not all that jolly. After the carnage we see Fugger kneeling in prayer, his ledger on the altar before him. Religion and capital remain in concord.

Before Forte's *Martin Luther* it seemed that documentary drama had reached the end of its development. Hochhuth, Kipphardt and Weiss have all abandoned it, perhaps in the age-old recognition that life's reality is not the reality of the theatre. Just as Naturalism came to the understanding that it had created a more refined form of illusion, so the attempts of documentary playwrights to come closer to the accurate depiction of real events resulted in what Max Frisch called 'second-degree illusion':

> To escape from the theatre of illusion rather than from a desire to be didactic, the playwright turns to the parable; in order then to escape from didacticism he turns further, as he imagines, and establishes illusion of the second degree.[34]

To view the illusion created by documentation as critically as the society from which the documents proceed, has been the achievement of Dieter Forte. It remains to be seen whether this will give documentary drama a new lease of life in Germany. Considering that the last five years have not added any significant contribution to the genre, it seems hardly likely to do so.

Notes to Chapter 8

1. R. Hinton Thomas and Keith Bullivant, *Literature in Upheaval*, Manchester University Press, Manchester, 1974, p. 92.
2. *Der Stellvertreter*, Rowohlt, Reinbek bei Hamburg, 1963, p. 124.
3. Ibid., p. 7.
4. Ibid., p. 9.
5. Ibid., p. 14.
6. Ibid., p. 16.
7. Ibid., pp. 29–30. Note the equation between Nazism and the diabolic, as already evident in Zuckmayer's *Des Teufels General*.
8. W. Mittenzwei, *Die vereinsamte Position eines Erfolgreichen. Der Weg des Dramatikers Rolf Hochhuth*, Volkstheater Rostock, Diskussionsheft 4, 1974, [p. 6].
9. *Der Stellvertreter*, p. 10.
10. *Soldaten*, Rowohlt, Reinbek bei Hamburg, 1967, p. 92.
11. Ibid., p. 33. Hochhuth's italics.

12. Ibid., p. 126.
13. Ibid., p. 127.
14. Heinar Kipphardt, *Joel Brand*, Suhrkamp, Frankfurt/Main, 1965, p. 103.
15. Heinar Kipphardt, *In der Sache J. Robert Oppenheimer*, Suhrkamp, Frankfurt/Main, 1964, p. 127.
16. Brecht, *Stücke*, Vol. III, Suhrkamp, Berlin, 1962, p. 188.
17. *Oppenheimer*, p. 34.
18. Ibid., p. 125.
19. Peter Weiss, *Dramen*, Vol. II, Suhrkamp, Frankfurt/Main, 1968, p. 464.
20. Ibid., p. 9.
21. Ibid., pp. 85–86.
22. Ibid. p. 86.
23. Ibid., pp. 198–99.
24. Ibid., p. 469.
25. Ibid., p. 469.
26. Ibid., p. 471.
27. *Theater heute*, Friedrich, Velber bei Hannover, May 1968, p. 66.
28. *Trotsky in Exile*, transl. by Geoffrey Skelton, Methuen, London, 1971, pp. 119–20 (*Trotzki im Exil*, Suhrkamp, Frankfurt/Main, 1970, pp. 140–41).
29. Hans Magnus Enzensberger, *Das Verhör von Habana*, Suhrkamp, Frankfurt/Main, 1970, p. 22.
30. Ibid., p. 152.
31. Ibid., p. 24.
32. *Dramen*, Vol. II, p. 467. In fairness to Enzensberger it must be admitted that he clearly states: '*The Havana Hearing* is neither a scenario nor a stage-play', but since it has enjoyed some popularity on the German stage in both East and West, being one of the ten most frequently produced contemporary plays in the 1970–71 season, it is reasonable to discuss it in terms of a stage-play.
33. Dieter Forte, *Martin Luther & Thomas Münzer oder Die Einführung der Buchhaltung*, Klaus Wagenbach, Berlin, 1971, p. 133.
34. Max Frisch, 'Illusion zweiten Grades', *Christ und Welt*, XXI, 3, 19. Jan. 1968.

9 The Theatre of the Common Man – the Volksstück

When one looks back over the corresponding development of post-war drama in Britain and Germany, one outstanding difference emerges. In the main, British drama has concerned itself with private conflicts, with analysing personal relationships in a domestic setting. German playwrights, on the other hand, have tended towards public debate, towards the discussion of wider political issues. This is understandable in a nation which has been at such pains to 'come to terms with the past' and which is divided into two states with fundamentally opposed political systems.

Nevertheless, tremendous interest has been shown by West German theatres in the work of Pinter, Osborne, Wesker and others, and the early plays of John Arden (*Live Like Pigs*, 1958, German premiere 1966 Staatstheater Stuttgart) and Edward Bond (*Saved*, 1965, German premiere 1967 Kammerspiele Munich, directed by Peter Stein) have had a profound influence on recent German playwriting. Now both German states are relaxing from their Cold War postures: the SPD's election to power with the consequent implementation of Brandt's policy of *détente*, and the increasing prosperity of East Germany since the building of the Wall in 1961 have been major factors in this. With the growing relaxation of wider political issues, the attention of German writers is now focussing on the situation of the common man in contemporary society.

A symptom of and a further influence on this new German theatre have been the revivals of the plays of Horváth and Fleisser. The dramas of Ödön von Horváth (1901–38), a German-speaking Austro-Hungarian, were banned during the Third Reich, and although they were occasionally performed after the war, above all in Austria, they were not fully 're-discovered' until the mid-sixties with productions of *Kasimir und Karoline* (1931) by the Schaubühne am Halleschen Ufer in 1964 and of *Geschichten aus dem Wienerwald* (*Tales from the Vienna Woods*, 1930) by the Kammerspiele Munich in 1966. More recently in 1968 and 1972, the Schaubühne am Halleschen Ufer has revived two plays of the Bavarian Marieluise Fleisser (b. 1901): *Pioniere in Ingolstadt* (*Pioneers in Ingolstadt*, 1929, rewritten 1968) and *Fegefeuer in Ingolstadt* (*Purgatory in Ingolstadt*, 1926, rewritten 1971). Each of these plays, like Brecht's *Puntila*, may be described as a

Volksstück (unsatisfactorily translatable as 'folk-play', cf. *Volkslied*, 'folk-song'), which Horváth described in the *Gebrauchsanweisung* (*Instructions for Use*) to his dramas as

> a play in which problems are dealt with and formulated in as popular ('volkstümlich') a manner as possible, questions of the common people, their simple worries, seen through the eyes of the people.[1]

To these literary influences must be added the more immediate effect of television. German theatre, more than most, has tended to talk in a language, High German, and act in a style that is (for want of a better word) 'theatrical', i.e. strikingly different from the language and behaviour of the man in the street. The realism and close-up technique of film and television have made the German theatregoer especially aware of dialogue and gesture that exist on stage and nowhere else. Significantly, most of the authors discussed in this chapter, notably Walser, Ziem, Fassbinder and Kroetz, have written for television.

Indeed, one of the most successful pieces about a domestic situation, which with 41 productions stands as the third most frequently staged contemporary German play in the last ten years, was originally written as a television script. This was Martin Walser's *Die Zimmerschlacht* (*Home-Front*, TV play 1962–63, stage-play 1967, premiere 1967 Kammerspiele Munich, directed by Fritz Kortner). In *Der Abstecher* (*The Detour*, 1961, premiere 1961 Kammerspiele Munich) Walser had already treated the theme of marital jealousy in a slightly absurdist manner (the husband, who has constructed an electric chair to execute his wife's former lover, forgives him over a beer). *Die Zimmerschlacht*, however, stands closer to Albee (*Who's Afraid of Virginia Woolf?* 1962) than to Ionesco. It seemed that Walser was happy to take up Kortner's suggestion of restyling his television script for the stage, because by the mid-sixties he was becoming aware of the inadequacies in the characterisation of his political plays:

> The figures of my parable plays tended to be reduced to specimens, to exemplars. That is to say, they did not enjoy a full range of consciousness. They had to fulfil too many political functions and I did not dare to enrich them with characteristics of a personal nature.[2]

The First Act of *Die Zimmerschlacht* shows Felix and Trude Fürst, having for rather devious reasons declined an invitation to a friend's party, forced to spend the evening together. Bored by each other's company, they continue to play their well-rehearsed roles, until Trude exposes a lie of Felix' and they resolve to be entirely honest for the rest of the evening. As a comment on the new morality of the middle-classes, Walser shows how disappointed Trude is when two supposed affairs of Felix turn out to have been harmless flirtations. Both of them have cherished longings to escape from their weary relationship; and, as they leave together for the party, each agrees to protect the other's weaknesses.

The Second Act, written on Kortner's instigation, takes place about fifteen years later. Once again Fritz makes the most of a story involving the blackmail of an eighteen-year-old schoolgirl, whom he claims to have photographed in the nude. Trude humours him by throwing a jealous scene, recognising that Felix needs these boasts to assure himself of his virility. Painful as the honesty of the First Act may have been, where marriage is described as an operation carried out by two surgeons on each other without anaesthetics, it still seems preferable to the empty routines of the Second Act. And yet it is these very routines that help to preserve their marriage. Their savage games derive from a curious kind of mutual understanding.

Edward Albee's *Who's Afraid of Virginia Woolf?* was also named as an important influence by Jochen Ziem, together with the plays of Pinter and the English Realist films of the fifties and sixties. Ziem (b. 1932) studied in East Germany and worked for a while with the Berliner Ensemble. He crossed to the West in 1956, and from 1961 to 1966 was editor-in-chief of Germany's leading consumer-magazine, *DM*. His first published play *Die Einladung* (*The Invitation*, premiere 1967 Schlosspark-Theater Berlin, directed by Hans Schweikart) sets a domestic dispute in an East Berlin apartment which overlooks the Wall. Thus, although personal relationships form the centre of interest, these are strongly conditioned by the political situation. So even in this genre we see the much stronger political awareness of German writers compared with their British counterparts.

The action takes place during the course of one night in the living-room of an engineer, Franz, and his wife. Since he is on the point of retiring, he has been invited to join his daughter, Hanna, in the West. The arrival of Hanna and her husband leads to a number of tense situations, especially with regard to her brother, Achim, who visibly suffers from his sense of being 'imprisoned' in East Germany. He is lazy and dispirited and somehow believes everything would go right for him in the West. Suddenly he disappears, and when he fails to return, the family assumes he must have escaped over the Wall. After a violent row Hanna and her husband drive off and Franz and his wife resign themselves to ending their days in the East. In the character of Franz, Ziem appears to have expressed many of his own hopes and disappointments about East Germany:

> Decide your own fate—that's what you were to do. Be able to learn what you wanted, work without fear, looking forward to the future and your old age without worries. How was I to know how things would turn out here? Could I have foreseen that? But I'd begin it all over again with the same hopes that I began with then.[3]

Ziem's next play, *Nachrichten aus der Provinz* (*News from the Provinces*, premiere 1967 Schiller-Theater Werkstatt Berlin) shows much stronger elements of the authentic *Volksstück*. It consists of eighteen separate scenes, nine of which were performed for the premiere, showing close-up portraits of situations in West Germany. We see two bored policemen intimidating passers-by, a removal man reminiscing about his adventures in Indo-China, a drunken worker pestering a negro and his white girl-friend with assurances about his tolerant attitudes, a policeman who has beaten up a neighbour's son confident that his conduct will be defended by his superiors, and so on. The style of brief anecdotal scenes with realistic but usually unnamed characters is reminiscent not only of Pinter's *Revue Sketches* but more particularly of Brecht's *Furcht und Elend des Dritten Reiches* (*Fear and Misery in the Third Reich*, American title: *The Secret Life of the Master-Race*, 1934–38). Here Brecht wrote 24 scenes about daily life under the Nazis. By deliberately echoing Brecht, Ziem is pointing to the failings of German society thirty years later. As the title suggests, he sees the Federal Republic as thoroughly provincial, with its greed, its prejudice, its complacency and above all its abuse of language. He regards his chief task as a dramatist to 'record authentic material about aspects of the world.' In fact, one of his scenes, *Es besteht Meinungsfreiheit* (*Free Speech Does Exist*), a formless political discussion among five men in a bar, was transcribed from an authentic tape-recording. Thus, although he insists that he has no didactic intent ('I don't want to offer any private coaching'), he has performed an invaluable service in being one of the first playwrights to reproduce modern German idiom accurately:

> The dramatist should . . . allow the stored-up clichés to erupt like a belch. Our colloquial language is full of unearthed treasures of this type.[4]

A similar study, this time of the petit-bourgeoisie of Hesse, was provided by Wolfgang Deichsel (b. 1939), one of the leaders of the Theater am Turm Frankfurt, in his *bleiwe losse* (*Leave It Be*, 1965, premiere 1971 Landestheater Darmstadt).

Ziem and Deichsel, although concerned with personal situations, treat their characters very much as political animals. This is even more evident in Martin Sperr. Sperr (b. 1944 in Lower Bavaria) became an actor in Munich at the age of 18. His three major plays form a trilogy about Bavarian life. The first of these is set in a village in 1948: *Jagdszenen aus Niederbayern* (*Hunting Scenes from Lower Bavaria*, premiere 1966 Theater der Freien Hansestadt Bremen). A number of plots and subplots reveal the attitudes of the inhabitants of Reinöd (a name suggesting 'Einöde', 'wilderness'). The central action is concerned with the persecution of a homosexual, Abram, by the petty-minded, unfeeling villagers. Although he would like to lead a 'normal' life with the girl who is expecting his child, Abram is driven by his mother's rejection and by social pressure into such a state of mental confusion that he murders the girl. All the villagers join in the ensuing hunt for the murderer, and after he is captured, they meet together in a celebration, agreeing to use the reward-money for a new church-organ—a cynical happy ending reminiscent of the final scene of Horváth's *Geschichten aus dem Wienerwald*. Another literary debt is to Büchner's *Woyzcek*, in the persecution of the simple outsider and the murder of the woman he loves.

In this first play, Sperr uses many devices with the sole intent of shocking the audience. There is not only a homosexual, but also a cripple and a mental defective; there is not only a murder, but also rape and suicide. These characters undoubtedly exist, these incidents undoubtedly occur in Bavarian villages, but the defence of plausibility is not enough for the theatre. By turning from the general to the particular, the realism of the *Volksstück* can easily end in banality or—as here—in sensationalism.

Like Ziem, Sperr seeks the meaning of a play in personal relationships:

When I go to the theatre I am not interested in the opinion of the author on some problem in the form of dialogue. I am interested in the relationships of the figures on stage to one another and to the action and in their opinions and how they have arrived at them.

In place of an artificial didactic style, Sperr insists on brutal realism:

I expect from the theatre the honesty to shit for real and not to show in what a jolly and delicate manner shitting can be avoided.[5]

Despite these provocative statements, the next stage of the trilogy is much more restrained. Where *Jagdszenen* owed an obvious debt to *Woyzeck*, it is *Romeo and Juliet* that is the progenitor of *Landshuter Erzählungen* (*Tales from Landshut*, premiere 1967 Kammerspiele Munich). He, Sorm, is the son of an old-fashioned builder who treats his workers badly and relies on his good name and good connections to remain prosperous. She, Sieglinde, is the daughter of a rival builder, whose methods are much more modern, who treats his workers relatively well but knows how to avoid trouble when one of his men is killed on a building-site. Sieglinde is already pregnant, but Sorm will not marry her until he owns his father's business. His father will not hand over the business because he is against the marriage, fearing that his rival would then take over both concerns. The deadlock is resolved when Sorm, threatened by disinheritance from his father, strangles him in a rage. Fortunately, the death seems like a heart-attack; so Sorm inherits the business, amalgamates with the rival company and marries Sieglinde. The only losers are the workers who are now faced by a virtual monopoly. Once again the play ends with an ironic idyll: as the now extended family sits sunning itself on the veranda, Sorm's mother reads from the horoscope. Happiness is predicted for both Sorm and Sieglinde.

In this portrayal of a provincial town in 1958, Sperr shows that the inhabitants may be more sophisticated but are certainly no less narrow-minded and ruthless than the villagers of his earlier play. The contradictions in their thinking are mercilessly exposed. Sorm's father relies on the possibility of a recession to intimidate his workers while trusting in the current boom to assure his prosperity. He also claims to be free of racial prejudice while displaying it at every turn:

I've got nothing against the Jews.—I was even against them being killed. It would have been enough if we'd got rid of them just by making life unpleasant for them.[6]

In a similarly perverted manner the landlady of the local public house urges her lover for the sake of 'morality' to divorce his wife:

You must get a divorce. It's immoral, what we're doing. . . . What do you want with a wife that's paralysed.[7]

Like Ziem, Sperr has a good ear for the clichés of modern colloquial German: Sorm's younger brother, a would-be student, reveals his intellectual snobbery in his use of foreign words, for example when he tells his parents that their quarrel with the rival firm is 'utterly jejune' ('eklatant niveaulos').[8] Sorm's mother also reveals how incapable she is of coping with reality when, after Sorm has strangled his father, she pathetically comments: 'If Otto had known that you wanted to kill him, he wouldn't have been so obstinate.'[9]

The third part of the trilogy now moves into the city and to 1969: *Münchner Freiheit* (*Munich Freedom*, premiere 1971 Schauspielhaus Düsseldorf). While *Jagdszenen* suffered from its sensationalism, *Münchner Freiheit* fails because it tries to treat too many broad themes at once, and so comes dangerously close to the clichés that Sperr himself is trying to expose. It deals with the conflict between capitalism and revolutionary students. The one liberal representative of capitalism, Ederer, commits a hideous suicide because of the infidelity of his wife. The protesting students are shown to be pathetic and directionless. At the end, Ederer's daughter, who had for a while lived in a student commune and taken part in the protests, is converted to capitalism. She will go to live with her mother's former lover, a town councillor. The final scene is again a party to celebrate improvements in business; capitalism is prospering.

In *Jagdszenen* a rape takes place on stage, in *Landshuter Erzählungen* Sorm and Sieglinde make love naked on a couch, and in *Münchner Freiheit* a student protest is accompanied by the flaunting of bare breasts. What in Sperr might be justified as a necessary component of his realism was soon to be exploited by lesser talents as a sound guarantee of box-office success. The most popular of these playwrights has been Wolfgang Bauer (b. 1941 in Graz, Austria). It is a sobering reflection on the operation of subsidised theatres in the West that the system has allowed his *Magic Afternoon* (premiere 1968 Landestheater Hanover) to be produced 34 times since 1968, thus placing it fourth equal alongside Handke's *Kaspar* in the table of most frequently staged contemporary German plays.

This one-act play purports to a certain authenticity by virtue of its extreme naturalism. Where Ziem and Sperr heighten their realism through selection, Bauer tries to give the impression of real events taking place on stage (a stage direction requires the director to make a fight-scene 'especially realistic'). Stage time corresponds to real time, and the dialogue is full of false starts, ellipses and banalities. But despite its naturalism, the action is pure melodrama.

Four drop-outs in their twenties try to overcome the boredom of a summer afternoon. They vaguely consider plans for a walk or a visit to the cinema, they smoke and drink, and Charly makes half-hearted attempts to write—but the only sentences that he can formulate are: 'Laziness is the driving force of this world' and 'Do as little as possible as quickly as possible.'[10] They play sex-games that are characterised by violence rather than tenderness, and one of the girls has to be taken to hospital with a broken nose. Finally, the two men get high on marijuana, giggle foolishly, kiss each other passionately and then torment the remaining girl in a kind of crazed 'bull-fight'. She seizes a knife, stabs one of the men to death and leaves abruptly. Charly goes and hides in a chest.

This hiding from reality is a physical expression of Charly's utter nihilism: 'Life is a habit like cigarette-smoking.'[11] As Botho Strauss, himself the author of a non-realistic play about the impossibility of communication in a capitalist society, *Die Hypochonder* (*The Hypochondriacs*, premiere 1972 Deutsches

Schauspielhaus Hamburg), commented:

> ... in the total passivity of the consumer, the existing hierarchy of culture is levelled out. They say Wittgenstein and mean Marlboro and vice versa.[12]

The same milieu is depicted in Bauer's next play, his first full-length drama, *Change* (*All Change*, premiere 1969 Volkstheater Vienna). It is the milieu described by Hilde Spiel as the 'muddy paddling-pool of a Viennese *bohème* that is as inarticulate as it is insignificant.'[13] It tells the story of an artist, Fery, who decides to manipulate the career of a young locksmith with artistic pretensions, Blasi Okopenko. The intention is to build him up with publicity and the collaboration of Fery's girl-friend and then to destroy him, perhaps even drive him to suicide; for Fery the process will be a huge artistic creation. In the course of the play, however, Blasi proves to be much tougher and more ruthless than Fery, and it is the young primitive who drives the intellectual to his death—he hangs himself in the lavatory. Apart from its nasty close, we are treated to the obligatory hash-party, sex-games and brutality (Fery's girl-friend has a miscarriage after being kicked in the stomach, a homosexual art-dealer has his face slashed with a broken glass).

Perhaps such things happen in artistic circles in Vienna. Fortunately, I am not in a position to know. What is clear, however, is that the violent incidents are crammed together without any analysis or compassion. The figures of Bauer's plays become as much functionaries of emotional shock as those of earlier political plays had been functionaries of political attitudes. When Fery commits suicide, we do not know why: it is more a bad attack of nerves than a psychologically motivated act. What Bauer does offer the middle-aged, middle-class theatre-goer is the titillation of partaking vicariously in the obscene and callous world of dilettante drop-outs together with the reassurance of the evil effects of cannabis and social nonconformity. No wonder Bauer is so popular in the municipal theatres of Western Germany. For my own part, I concur with Harold Hobson's verdict on the British premiere of Bauer's *Gespenster* (*Ghosts*, premiere 1974 Kammerspiele Munich):

> I would not have believed that a play so crowded with lurid action and physical flaunting could be so dull. The four-letter words, the endless drinking, the interminable, solemn, and three-quarters sozzled chatter about art induce a feeling of intolerable boredom. One totters from the theatre exhausted with fatigue.[14]

Regrettably, other young Austrian playwrights, presumably attracted by Bauer's success, have tried to imitate his formula. Harald Sommer (b. 1935 in Styria) wrote a similar style of drama in dialect, *A unhamlich schtorka obgong* (*A Gruesomely Strong Exit*, premiere 1970 Schauspielhaus Graz). After the realism of the introductory hash-party the incidents become more and more improbable, until the 'heroine' is saved by a *deus ex machina*. Peter Turrini (b. 1944 in Carinthia) began writing in the same sensationalist vein, e.g. *rozznjogd* (*Rat Hunt*, premiere 1971 Volkstheater Vienna) and *Sauschlachten* (*Slaughter of the Pigs*, premiere 1972 Kammerspiele Munich). Mercifully, Turrini has now turned to adaptations of Goldoni and Beaumarchais. His version of Beaumarchais' *The Marriage of Figaro*, entitled *Der tollste Tag* (*The Most Crazy Day*, premiere 1972 Landestheater Darmstadt), has been particularly popular.

One of the most promising writers of the *Volksstück* is also one of the youngest and the most prolific. Franz Xaver Kroetz (b. 1946 in Munich) has had innumerable odd jobs—as chauffeur, lorry-driver, male-nurse, banana-cutter and actor. His first plays also tend to rely on shocking incidents for dramatic effect, but they cut much deeper than the phantasmagoria of Bauer. This was seen clearly in public reaction to his *Heimarbeit* (*Homeworker*, premiere 1971 Kammerspiele Munich). At the premiere there were chanting crowds protesting on the street outside the theatre. The police on guard admitted the audience singly, and even then stink-bombs were let off in the auditorium. Twice the performance was brought to a halt, but in the midst of the rumpus many of those present were aware that an important new talent had arrived in the German theatre.

The reasons for the violence of public reaction are not hard to discover. True, it is a nasty little story: Willy, condemned by an accident to work at home, learns that his wife is pregnant by another man. They attempt an unsuccessful abortion with a knitting needle. The baby is born deformed and cries all the time; so Willy eventually murders it. But the horror of the story is not much worse than moments of *Change*. The difference is that Kroetz draws characters from the very lowest social stratum; what in Bauer is a perverse game, is here a matter of utter seriousness. A public prepared to confront the spectacle of cannabis-crazed drop-outs committing violent acts were genuinely shocked when faced with real brutality not at the fringe but at the core of society. The implications were far less palatable.

This was particularly so when Kroetz turned to a rustic setting, as in *Wildwechsel* (*Wild Animals Crossing*, premiere 1971 Dortmunder Schauspiel) and *Stallerhof* (*Staller Farm*, premiere 1972 Malersaal, Deutsches Schauspielhaus Hamburg). The latter play has also caused its share of trouble: a teacher in Tirol was dismissed for organising a reading of it at her school. Traditionally, the harshest naturalism has tended towards sentimentality about peasants. There is an implied belief in Gerhart Hauptmann's naturalist plays, for example, that suggests that all would be right in the world if only the Industrial Revolution had not taken place. It is a comforting, apolitical attitude that dismisses the need for change by accepting industrial society as an unalterable evil. But, like Sperr, Kroetz shows that 'old-German' peasant stock is every bit as corrupt as their 'uprooted' cousins in the towns.

Stallerhof tells how Sepp, a farm-worker, seduces Beppi, the young mentally-defective daughter of Staller, the farmer for whom he works. The enraged Staller shoots Sepp's dog and sends Sepp away. Frau Staller contemplates an abortion but changes her mind. The play ends as the labour pains begin. With extreme compassion, Kroetz depicts the gentle love between the older man and the child-like girl. We first encounter them at work together with Sepp telling her a story of adventure. In the next scene he sits on a lavatory and masturbates. It is a crude image, but by no means gratuitous, expressing as it does his frustration and isolation. He achieves pathetic satisfaction of his desires with Beppi, but their relationship is soon discovered and condemned. Sepp is attacked by Beppi's father:

STALLER: You must be the biggest swine I know.

(*Pause*)

STALLER: A child under age, what's mentally retarded. I'm lost for words.
SEPP: Didn't mean it. I swear.
STALLER: Couldn't you have found someone else? You don't do anything in the house you work in, specially when it's a child.
SEPP: I never had the nerve. Nowhere.
STALLER: Why?
SEPP: Not saying.[15]

The only glimmer of light in the narrow-minded reaction of the parents occurs when the mother relents from attempting the abortion and so allows Beppi, a child herself, to give birth to a child.

Much of the play consists of pauses for which Kroetz prescribes exact timings in the opening stage-directions. These, together with the minimal dialogue, reflect the inarticulacy of his characters. Kroetz shows that one of the greatest deprivations of the poor is their inability to communicate. By giving them the opportunity of expression, by allowing his audience to understand the reality behind events normally only familiar through newspaper articles, he is committing a political act.

This political commitment has now become more conscious. He admits that from about Autumn 1971 he had been disturbed 'by the extreme nature' of his plays and recognised that 'the social commitment that is contained in them does not proceed from analysis of society by the author but from horror and anger at the way things are.'[16] In 1972 he joined the German Communist Party, and in a recent interview in the East German monthly *Theater der Zeit* he declared: 'Acts of violence do not form the subject of my one-act plays but the social and mental disintegration which produces acts of violence.'[17]

After the violence of his early plays Kroetz is now searching for a more effective means of expressing his political viewpoint. He has worked on adaptations of Hebbel's dramas, *Maria Magdalena* (premiere 1973 Städtische Bühnen Heidelberg) and *Agnes Bernauer*, in an effort to develop a dramatic style that can deal with socially more powerful figures than those of his *Volksstücke*. Meanwhile his plays about common people have developed new strength, e.g. *Dolomiten-stadt Lienz* (*Lienz, Town in the Dolomites*) and *Wunschkonzert* (*Request Programme*), both premiered in the 1972/73 season. The most popular of these has been *Oberösterreich* (*Morecambe*, premiere 1972 Städtische Bühnen Heidelberg). There are two characters: Anni and Heinz. After a number of scenes characterising their petit-bourgeois marriage, Anni reveals that she is pregnant. Heinz is not at all pleased and insists on an abortion. Once again one of Kroetz' favourite themes recurs, but this time it is treated with much greater restraint and between characters who show some understanding and respect for each other. Financially, they regard it as almost impossible for them to support a child, but Anni still refuses to terminate her pregnancy. The situation worsens when Heinz loses his licence for drunken driving and so must give up his job as a delivery-man. In the last scene we learn that the firm has given him temporary alternative employment and that he has willingly resigned himself to the birth of his child. Anni reads an item from the newspaper: in Upper Austria a man murdered his wife in desperation because she refused to agree to an abortion.

HEINZ: It takes all types. Same sort of thing as us. We know what it's like.
ANNI: Don't be silly, you're not a murderer.
HEINZ: That's the difference.
ANNI: Exactly.[18]

In this exchange, Kroetz shows not only the precariousness of Heinz' and Anni's present idyll but also how the smallest additional pressure, the tiniest reduction in their love and companionship might have turned the action towards the horror of the earlier plays. Contented as they are in this final scene, their problems are really only about to begin. In the style of Horváth's ironical endings, the piece closes with Heinz playing a Viennese melody on his accordion.

By moving from the *Lumpenproletariat* to the petit-bourgeoisie, Kroetz can allow his characters greater articulacy. But their language is conditioned by advertising and the mass-media, and they frequently communicate in the style of the brochure or the television programme:

ANNI: It might be really nice, a trip on the steamer. Perhaps an unforgettable experience, what with Easter bathing itself in the warm glow of the Spring sunshine.
HEINZ: But they said on telly there's a new ice-age on the way.
ANNI: Why?
HEINZ: A new ice-age is approaching. That's what a meteorologist said.[19]

Apart from the political implications of their conditioned linguistic style, Kroetz also takes great care to detail the economic situation of the couple. In the scene where Heinz and Anni discuss whether they can afford to have the child, we watch them making an exact balance of their monthly income and expenditure. Since Anni will have to stop working, sacrifices will have to be made: he is prepared to give up 'his' car, she 'her' television, but there is still little enough left:

HEINZ: £64·55 for three people, for food and clothing.

(*Does a sum*)

70 pence for each of us per day.

(*Pause*)

It's not much.
ANNI: No.
HEINZ: Seeing as we've taken away everything that gives us any pleasure in life.[20]

Without any heavy-handed political comment, Kroetz has drawn a precise and compassionate picture of the predicament of the small man in today's consumer society. Much is achieved by avoiding didacticism, and Anni's last words are more insistent than lengthy polemic:

> The child . . . must grow up different to us. Else there's no sense in anything at all. Right from the start.[21]

The most popular recent *Volksstück* has been Mühl's *Rhein-promenade* (*Promenade by the Rhine*, 1971–72, premiere 1973 Wupper-taler Bühnen, directed by Arno Wüstenhöfer). Karl Otto Mühl[22] (b. 1923 in Nuremberg) has spent most of his life working in industry and has only recently turned to playwriting. Like Kroetz, Mühl does not claim a specific political message for his *Volksstücke*; his writing is a product of compassion: 'I am outraged when men suffer injustice, when men are deformed.[23] Like *Stallerhof*, this play deals with the love of an older man, Fritz, for a mentally retarded girl. The setting is now the Rhineland, Fritz is already 77 and the girl is a coloured kitchen-maid at a hospital. Fritz' daughter, who suffers from living with a weak and childish husband, seeks to destroy their relationship. When Fritz dies, the daughter ensures that the girl does not even keep the little money that he had given her on his death-bed. The favourite themes recur: the lack of understanding and narrowness of vision, the crushing of a love that is different, the lack of communication. Repeatedly, one character says to another, 'you're not listening' or 'I can't listen to all that', and the way in which the dialogue often consists of parallel monologues is reminiscent of Pinter.

Already with Mühl's *Rheinpromenade*, the *Volksstück* shows signs of parodying itself, of slipping into the horrific or the sentimental. Instead of fulfilling Horvath's prescription that the *Volksstück* should present 'questions of the common people . . . seen through the eyes of the people', it all too often offers a view from above which is shocked or condescending. 'Popular drama' easily becomes drama of the élite.

Significantly, Kroetz and Turrini appear to have abandoned the *Volksstück*, and other writers, while coming under the influence of the genre, have stood aside from its realism. Thus although Rolf Hochhuth's *Die Hebamme* (*The Midwife*, premiere 1972 Kammerspiele Munich, Schauspielhaus Zurich and Deutsches Theater Göttingen) deals with a contemporary situation in West Germany, it derives essentially from traditional comedy, pursuing laughter rather than realism. Rainer Werner Fassbinder (b. 1946), former director at the Antiteater in Munich but now best known as a film-director, introduced a comic-strip figure into his play, *Blut am Hals der Katze* (*Blood on the Cat's Neck*, premiere 1972 Städtische Bühnen Nuremberg). Phoebe Zeitgeist comes from another planet to learn the language of contemporary society. His *Bremer Freiheit* (*Bremen Coffee*, premiere 1971 Concordia, Theater der Freien Hansestadt Bremen), while dealing with the topical issue of women's rights, is in fact a period piece.

The recent development in the *Volksstück* has been towards the adoption of more overtly political themes. The most successful of these has been Heinrich Henkel's *Eisenwichser* (*The Painters*, premiere 1970 Basler Theater) which was produced on 24 different stages in its first two seasons. Henkel (b. 1937 in Karlsruhe) is a trained painter and decorator, who now lives as a free-lance writer in Basle. *Eisenwichser* does not only show us the proletarian; it takes us into his place of work.

Volker, a young painter of 20, is given a job alongside the 57-year-old Lötscher. Lötscher has already spent the last thirty years of his working-life painting the mass of pipes in the underground tunnel of a factory. He is a loyal employee who takes a pride in his work. Stiff in the joints and inclined to talk to himself after such prolonged isolation, he has learnt to accept his soulless existence without question, even obediently thanking his boss for his pay-packet. Volker, on the other hand, displays all the signs of youthful rebellion, 'forgets' to thank the boss for his pay and argues with Lötscher about the older man's fastidiousness.

The Second Act takes place five months later. Volker has by now settled down completely to the work, and the vociferous exchanges of the First Act have become decidedly laconic. Without their knowing it, the ventilators break down and they are gradually affected by the fumes of their paint. Coughing and giggling, they reach a state of total intoxication, falling about and splashing paint wildly. For a while the spectator can revel in the anarchy of the situation, but soon enough Volker is trying to press a brush into the hand of the unconscious Lötscher, encouraging him to paint 'just another metre'. The conditioning has worked well; in twenty years Volker will be another Lötscher. This bleak and clearly authentic description of industrial working-conditions opened up new perspectives for middle-class audiences and raised many questions about employment in a technological age.

The same sort of questions are posed in a play by the East German Ulrich Plenzdorf (b. 1934), *Die neuen Leiden des jungen W.* (*The New Sorrows of Young W.*, premiere 1972 Landestheater Halle, directed by Horst Schönemann). The title of this drama which has enjoyed considerable success on both sides of the German border, alludes to Goethe's Storm and Stress *novelle*, *Die Leiden des jungen Werthers* (*The Sorrows of Young Werther*, 1774). In Goethe's story Werther loves a married woman. He is convinced that he could offer her more than her stiff and formal husband is able to, but rather than disturb their domestic peace, he goes off and blows out his brains. The new W. is Edgar Wibeau, a young misfit who leaves home to live in a semi-ruined building where he gets to know the young teacher from the neighbouring kindergarten. Like the Charlotte of Goethe's tale, she marries a rather tedious, settled man, although she is clearly attached to the easygoing nonconformist Edgar. In Plenzdorf's version the young hero does not shoot himself. He has been taken up into a tolerant collective of decorators who do their best to reform him and turn him into a useful member of their team. In turn, Edgar tries to develop an efficient paint-spray that will increase their productivity. While working on his invention he kills himself accidentally. In a surprisingly frank way Plenzdorf discusses the difficulty encountered by the individualistic type in adapting to the demands of the collective society.

In this very promising new play from East Germany a possible new direction for the *Volksstück* is seen. The danger with the anecdotal character of Ziem's short scenes or Kroetz' one-act plays is that they deal with symptoms and not causes. Plenzdorf's drama shows one possibility of relating the individual case to a wider concern, of bringing together questions that are political as well as personal.

Notes to Chapter 9

1. Cit. Herbert Gamper, 'Horváth und die Folgen—das Volksstück?', *Theater 1971*, Friedrich, Velber bei Hannover, p. 73.
2. Cit. Henning Rischbieter, 'Genre-Bilder', *Theater heute*, January 1968, p. 32.
3. *Theater heute*, July 1967, p. 55.
4. Jochen Ziem, 'Was gesprochen wird, was auf die Bühne quillt', *Theater heute*, July 1967, p. 47f.
5. 'Junge Autoren und das Theater', *Theater 1967*, p. 53.
6. *Theater 1967*, p. 82.
7. Ibid., p. 85.
8. Ibid., p. 85.
9. Ibid., p. 87.
10. *Theater heute*, October 1968, p. 60.
11. Ibid., p. 60.
12. Botho Strauss, 'Das Ende einer Clique', *Theater heute*, October 1968, p. 57.
13. *Theater heute*, November 1971, p. 16.
14. Harold Hobson, 'In the quicksands', *The Sunday Times*, 20 July 1975, p. 27.
15. *Theater 1971*, p. 82.
16. Kroetz, 'Ich sässe lieber in Bonn im Bundestag', *Theater heute*, February 1973, p. 48f.
17. *Theater der Zeit*, January 1975, p. 54.
18. *Theater heute*, February 1973, p. 60.
19. Ibid., p. 56.
20. Ibid., p. 59.
21. Ibid., p. 60.
22. Karl Otto Mühl is not to be confused with the Austrian Otto Mühl, who with Herbert Nitsch and Günter Brus has been involved in a particularly nasty form of experimental theatre which involves smearing naked women with animal blood and faeces.
23. Mühl, 'Gesehene Realität betrifft immer auch andere', *Theater 1973*, p. 165.

10 Conclusion

It is not easy to generalise about thirty years of theatre in four German-speaking nations, one of which has an entirely different social system from the other three. What one can point to, however, are the consistently 'public' themes of most post-war German plays. Even where they are not overtly political, they usually have much greater social relevance than most contemporary drama favoured by the English stage (e.g. Albee, Pinter, Beckett). It is characteristic that Frisch in his most domestic play, *Biografie*, introduces Kürmann's membership of the Communist Party, and Dürrenmatt's adaptation of *Dance of Death* in *Play Strindberg* transforms a domestic situation into a generalised vision of economic exploitation. Again, there have been a number of plays set in mental hospitals, notably Dürrenmatt's *Die Physiker*, Weiss' *Marat/Sade* and—in part—*Hölderlin*, Walser's *Der schwarze Schwan* and Karl Wittlinger's popular *Kennen Sie die Milchstrasse?* (*Do You Know the Milky Way?* premiere 1956 Bühnen der Stadt Cologne). Significantly, in each case the asylum-setting has been used as a social and political metaphor, never to explore the phenomenon of insanity.

Recent German drama does not merely remove the fourth wall; it knocks down the other three as well, showing human action in a wider social context. When German writers wish to turn to more private themes, they take up the novel or lyric poetry. If all the plays in the German language were totally destroyed tomorrow, all of the following playwrights would continue to be read for their other literary achievements: Brecht, Dürrenmatt, Frisch, Handke, Weiss, Borchert, Enzensberger, Grass, Siegfried Lenz and Walser.

The reasons for the predominance of political and social drama are not hard to find. Germany and Austria suffered the infestation of Fascist ideology with its extreme political oppression, militarism and genocide, and Switzerland was something more than a mere onlooker. Cynically, one may also observe that Germany lost the war. The inescapable impulse towards an analysis of political cause and effect, towards coming to terms with the past, naturally determined the course drama was to take. Even when the ghosts of the past had been more or less laid, the continuing division of Germany into a capitalist and a Communist state kept political considerations to the fore. By contrast, the potential subjects for the political dramatist in Britain are sparse: Northern Ireland is still too topical and too complex, and there is not much mileage to be got out of the Common Market or Home Rule for Wales.

As may therefore be expected, the greatest contribution by Germany to the theatre of the world has been in the field of political drama. Despite the surrealistic elements in Dürrenmatt and some of the plays of Hildesheimer, Grass and Dorst, the Theatre of the Absurd never took root in Germany. And as we have seen in discussion of the *Volksstück*, the 'kitchen-sink' naturalism of domestic scenes has been only a recent introduction—under the influence of trends from Britain rather than the reverse.

Curiously, while the German theatre is catching up with an out-moded English theatrical style, British theatre has absorbed more and more from a major German source: Bert Brecht. Ronald Hayman goes so far as to say that Brecht 'has exerted more influence than anyone else not only on playwriting, design and style in production, but on our whole approach to the theatre.'[1] Certainly, the visit of the Berliner Ensemble to London in 1956, the year of Brecht's death, was a major theatrical event. The Ensemble performed *Der kaukasische Kreidekreis*, *Mutter Courage* and *Pauken und Trompeten*, and astonished English audiences with their adventurousness, attention to detail and obvious political commitment. John Arden admitted how affected he had been on seeing *Mutter Courage*, and his work clearly owes a considerable debt to Brecht. The same is true of Edward Bond and to a lesser extent of John Osborne. Indeed, all three seem to have 'jumped' from early realistic writing to a more Brechtian style: Arden's *Live Like Pigs* (1958) was followed by *Serjeant Musgrave's Dance* (1959); Bond moved from *Saved* (1965) to *Early Morning* (1968); and Osborne left the conventional dramaturgy of *Look Back in Anger* (1956) for *The Entertainer* (1957) and *Luther* (1961).

There has also been a correspondingly 'Brechtian' influence on design, which has generally abandoned fussy realism in favour of austere and evocative sets; on acting, which has moved from Stanislavskian introspection to a greater awareness of characters as social representatives; and on directors like Peter Hall, William Gaskill and Max Stafford-Clark. I have set 'Brechtian' in inverted commas, because it is impossible to tell how much of all this would have happened anyway through reaction against established styles, economic pressures and the effect of television. Like all successful influences, Brecht's came when the time was ripe for it.

It must be remembered too that while 'Brechtian' is a favourite term in the British theatre, very few people have actually read him. Indeed, the first English translation of his writings on the theatre did not appear until 1964. By that time it would probably have been too late to destroy many of the misconceptions that now prevail about Brecht, the most popular of which is that 'he is against emotion.' I once endured an unbelievably dismal West End production of *The Threepenny Opera* and was further dismayed the next Sunday to read a leading critic's comment that 'it was perhaps not gloomy enough for Brecht fans'.

It is sobering to reflect that the most genuinely Brechtian of our playwrights, Arden and Bond, have found little favour with the British public, and in fact we are still a long way from having fully understood, much less explored the important ideas that Brecht has proposed. Against Hayman's confident assertion of Brecht's importance for the post-war British theatre we may set Albert Hunt's words:

> ... there is a complete absence of any intellectual tradition or any sense of continuity in the British theatre itself. Fashions come and go in our theatre: the theatre of the absurd is followed by the angry young men, who are followed by the theatre of cruelty. In such a situation, Brecht becomes a fad invented by Kenneth Tynan in the 1950s: he came and went like the rest.[2]

While Brecht's successors on the Continent, Palitzsch, Wekwerth and Heyme in Germany, Planchon in France, and Strehler in Italy, continue to investigate and extend his ideas, here in Britain we have to wait for the spasmodic appearance of a piece like the Joint Stock Company's production of David Hare's *Fanshen*. And by all accounts, things in America are worse.

Apart from Brecht, there was for many years little happening in German theatre that might have been internationally significant. As an indicator, in the period 1951–61 there were only three Broadway productions of German plays, one that had been written in 1942, Hochwälder's *The Strong Are Lonely*, one of limited literary merit, Wittlinger's *Do You Know the Milky Way?*, and only one significant example of post-war German drama, Dürrenmatt's *The Visit*. But just as France had enjoyed a theatrical renaissance in the nineteen-forties, and Britain experienced hers in the fifties, so the turn of German-speaking nations came in the sixties. Frisch's *The Fire-Raisers* and *Andorra* and Dürrenmatt's *The Physicists* rapidly achieved international fame. Then in the mid-sixties two German plays detonated on the stages of the world: Hochhuth's *The Representative*, which, in Dürrenmatt's words, 'deals with the last myth there is, the infallibility of the Pope';[3] and Weiss' *Marat/Sade*, a work so rich and exciting that Peter Brook could write of it:

> Starting with its title, everything about this play is designed to crack the spectator on the jaw, then douse him with ice-cold water, then force him to assess intelligently what has happened to him, then give him a kick in the balls, then bring him back to his senses again.[4]

The Representative and Weiss' next play, *The Investigation*, established Germany as the major source of documentary drama, and Kipphardt's *In the Matter of J. Robert Oppenheimer*, Grass' *The Plebeians Rehearse the Uprising* and Hochhuth's *Soldiers* also found their way onto many of the world's stages. The documentary drama of Germany has unquestionably been the most important influence to emerge since Brecht and like him has had widespread influence on the British theatre. This ranges from the precise research which Arden has carried out for much of his recent work to the local documentaries presented by Peter Cheeseman at the Victoria Theatre, Stoke-on-Trent, and the documentary revues of numerous fringe groups. With television obviously playing an important role in this area, it is difficult to isolate the influence that has come from Germany, but it would be equally difficult to deny it.

Since the boom in documentary drama there has been little of significance that has emerged from Germany. The latest plays of Dürrenmatt and Frisch are performed out of respect rather than conviction. Some small theatre-groups misguidedly nibble at the forbidden fruits of Wolfgang Bauer. Peter Hacks remains in hideous neglect. Only Peter Handke has caused ripples of interest, especially with *Offending the Audience* and *Kaspar*, but it has been an intellectual's response rather than general public reception.

In fact, if one looks over the most frequently produced contemporary German plays of the last ten years, one sees that the German-language theatre is sharing the stagnation that seems general in the world. Of the ten leading plays only Handke's *Kaspar* is of any real importance. The history of twentieth-century drama will easily be written without even mentioning the rest.

Perhaps some of this is due to the inflexible structure of municipal and state theatres. One simply cannot know whether there are fine writers, directors and actors who have rejected, or have been rejected by the system. All one can say is that they surely stand a better chance in Germany than in Britain or the United States.

There are signs too that the structures are loosening (another irony, when British theatres are depending more and more on state support and therefore drawing ever closer to state control). The 'Fringe' has been gnawing away at the 'Establishment' and it may be that the German theatre will dare to become more generally experimental. There are still some good writers about: the creative powers of Hacks, Weiss and Dorst seem by no means exhausted, and there is surely still much to be expected of younger writers like Handke, Kroetz, Forte and Plenzdorf.

For a theatre which had been brought to a virtual standstill by Nazi barbarism, to have produced two major influences in thirty years is not a bad record. Given the intelligence, dedication and financial security of those who work in the German theatre, the third will not be long in coming.

Notes to Chapter 10

1. 'Brecht in the English Theatre', *The German Theatre*, ed. R. Hayman, Wolff, London, 1975, p. 201.
2. 'A Permanent State of Re-Invention', *The Times Educational Supplement*, July 25, 1975.
3. *Dramaturgisches und Kritisches*, Arche, Zurich, 1972, p. 230.
4. *Marat/Sade*, Calder & Boyars, London, 1965, [p. 6].

Chart of Important Productions 1944-75

Year	Event	Title	Author
1944	Sept 1. All theatres closed in Germany and Austria	*The Skin of Our Teeth*	Wilder
1945	Re-opening of Dt Th East Berlin, Schloss-park-Th West Berlin (under BOLESLAW BARLOG), Burgth Vienna	*Nun singen sie wieder* *Nathan der Weise*	Frisch Lessing
1946	GUSTAF GRÜND-GENS joins newly renovated Dt Th East Berlin, opens with:	*Die chinesische Mauer* *Des Teufels General* *Die Illegalen* *Capt. B's Conversion* *King Oedipus*	Frisch Zuckmayer Weisenborn Shaw Sophocles
1947	BRECHT leaves USA for Switzerland GRÜNDGENS reopens Schsph Düsseldorf	*Draussen vor der Tür* *Es steht geschrieben*	Borchert Dürrenmatt
1948	BRECHT writes *Kleines Organon für das Theater*	*Antigone* *Puntila* *Der öffentliche A* *Der Blinde* *The Flies*	Sophocles/ Brecht Brecht Hochwälder Dürrenmatt Sartre
1949	BRECHT goes to East Berlin to found Berliner Ens with his wife HELENE WEIGEL	*Mutter Courage* *Puntila* *Romulus der Grosse* *Faust I*	Brecht Brecht Dürrenmatt Goethe
1950	HEINZ HILPERT opens Dt Th Göttingen HARRY BUCKWITZ becomes *Intendant* of St Bn Frankfurt	*Der Hofmeister* *Der Gesang im Feuerofen* *Don Carlos*	Lenz/Brecht Zuckmayer Schiller

The following abbreviations are used:

Bn — Bühne(n); Dt — Deutsches; Ens — Ensemble;
Ksp — Kammerspiele; Schsph — Schauspielhaus; St — Städtische;
Th — Theater; Long titles have also been shortened.

Theatre	*Director*	*Cast*
Schsph Zurich		
Schsph Zurich	Horwitz	
Dt Th Berlin		
Schsph Zurich	Steckel	
Schsph Zurich	Hilpert	Knuth
Hebbelth Berlin		
Dt Th Berlin	Gründgens	
Dt Th Berlin	Gründgens	
Ksp Hamburg		
Schsph Zurich	Horwitz	
Chur	Brecht/Neher	Weigel
Schsph Zurich	Hirschfeld/Brecht	Steckel
Neues Th Stuttgart		
Stadtth Basel		
Hebbelth Berlin	Fehling	
Dt Th Berlin	Brecht/Engel	Weigel
Berliner Ens	Brecht/Engel	Steckel
Stadtth Basel		Horwitz
St Bn Düsseldorf	Gründgens	Gründgens
Berliner Ens	Brecht/Neher	
Dt Th Göttingen	Hilpert	
Hebbelth Berlin	Kortner	Kortner

Year	Event	Title	Author
1951	BARLOG opens Schiller-Th West Berlin MANFRED WEKWERTH and PETER PALITZSCH join Berliner Ens ERWIN PISCATOR returns from USA	*Die Mutter* *Graf Öderland* *Samba*	Brecht Frisch Becher
1952		*Die Gewehre der Carrar* *Ehe des Mississippi* *S dringend gesuch* *Maria Stuart*	Brecht Dürrenmatt Kipphardt Schiller
1953		*Don Juan* *Engel kommt nach B.* *Katzgraben* *Donadieu*	Frisch Dürrenmatt Strittmatter Hochwälder
1954	Berliner Ens moves to Th am Schiffbauer- damm, wins 1st prize at Théâtre des Nations Paris HANS LIETZAU joins Schiller-Th Berlin	*Kauk. Kreidekreis*	Brecht
1955	GRÜNDGENS be- comes *Intendant* of Dt Schsph Hamburg KARL HEINZ STROUX becomes *Intendant* of Schsph Düsseldorf DÜRREN- MATT publishes his *Theaterprobleme*	*E des Zeitalters* *Die Dorfstrasse* *Winterschlacht* *Das kalte Licht* *War and Peace*	Hacks Matusche Becher Zuckmayer Tolstoy/Piscator
1956	Death of BRECHT Berliner Ens visits London	*Besuch der alten Dame* *Die Tage der Commune* *Schlacht bei Lobositz* *Thomas Chatterton* *Philemon und Baukis*	Dürrenmatt Brecht Hacks Jahnn Ahlsen
1957	Completion of Mannheim Nationalth	*Leben des Galilei* *Gesichte der S. Machard* *Furcht und Elend* *Die Herberge*	Brecht Brecht/Feucht- wanger Brecht Hochwälder
1958		*Biedermann* *Müller von Sanssouci* *Der Lohndrücker* *Pastorale* *Der grosse Verzicht*	Frisch Hacks Müller Hildesheimer Schneider
1959		*Arturo Ui* *Die heilige Johanna* *The Rhinoceroses* *The Dumb Waiter*	Brecht Brecht Ionesco Pinter
1960	PETER PALITZSCH leaves East Germany for the West	*Sorgen und die Macht* *Die Kurve* *Gesellschaft im Herbst* *The Caretaker*	Hacks Dorst Dorst Pinter

Theatre	Director	Cast
Berliner Ens	Brecht	Weigel
Schsph Zurich	Steckel	Knuth
Th in der Josefstadt Vienna		
Berliner Ens	Brecht	Weigel
Ksp Munich	Schweikart	
Dt Th Berlin		
Schillerth Berlin	Fehling	Held, Flickenschild
Schsph Zurich	Wälterlin	
Ksp Munich		
Berliner Ens	Brecht	
Burgth Vienna		
Berliner Ens	Brecht	Busch, Weigel
Ksp Munich		
Ksp Dt Th Berlin		
Berliner Ens	Brecht/Wekwerth	
Dt Schsph Hamburg	Gründgens	
Schiller-Th Berlin	Piscator	
Schsph Zurich	Wälterlin	Giehse, Knuth
Karl-Marx-Stadt	Besson/Wekwerth	
Dt Th Berlin		
Dt Schsph Hamburg	Gründgens	
Ksp Munich		
Berliner Ens	Brecht/Engel	Busch
St Bn Frankfurt	Buckwitz	
Berliner Ens		
Burgth Vienna		
Schsph Zurich	Wälterlin	
Ksp Dt Th Berlin		
St Th Leipzig		
Ksp Munich		
Bregenz		Ens of Burgth Vienna
Berliner Ens	Wekwerth/Palitzsch	Schall
Dt Schsph Hamburg	Gründgens	
Schsph Düsseldorf	Stroux	
St Bn Frankfurt		
Senftenberg		
Bn der Hansestadt	Lübeck	
Nationalth Mannheim		
Schsph Düsseldorf		

Year	Event	Title	Author
1961		*Andorra*	Frisch
		Frau Flinz	Baierl
		Zeit der Schuldlosen	Lenz
		Der Abstecher	Walser
		Grosse Schmährede	Dorst
		Die bösen Köche	Grass
		The Hostage	Behan
1962	ERWIN PISCATOR	*Die Physiker*	Dürrenmatt
	becomes 1st *Intendant*	*Eiche und Angora*	Walser
	of Freie Volksbn	*Die Tage der Commune*	Brecht
	West Berlin Founding	*Andorra*	Frisch
	of Schaubn am Halles-	*Der Hund des Generals*	Kipphardt
	chen Ufer Berlin	*Don Carlos*	Schiller
	Death of CASPAR	*Peace*	Aristophanes/
	NEHER		Hacks
1963	LIETZAU leaves	*Der Stellvertreter*	Hochhuth
	Schillerth Berlin	*Herkules*	Dürrenmatt
	Death of GRÜNDGENS	*Der Unbelehrbare*	Wünsche
	Freie Volksbn moves to	*Herr Krott*	Walser
	new building		
	Completion of new		
	theatre for St Bn		
	Frankfurt		
1964	LIETZAU joins	*Marat/Sade*	Weiss
	Residenzth Munich		
	Death of HEINZ	*Coriolan*	Shakespeare/
	HILPERT		Brecht
		Oppenheimer	Kipphardt
		Der schwarze Schwan	Walser
		Kasmir und Karoline	Horváth
1965		*Die Ermittlung*	Weiss
		Marat/Sade	Weiss
		Joel Brand	Kipphardt
		Helm	Michelsen
		Der Drache	Schwarz
		Three Sisters	Chekhov
1966	Death of PISCATOR	*Der Meteor*	Dürrenmatt
	PALITZSCH senior	*Publikumsbeschimpfung*	Handke
	producer in Stuttgart	*Selbstbezichtigung*	Handke
	Completion of	*Jagdszenen aus N.*	Sperr
	Wuppertal Schsph	*Plebejer proben den A.*	Grass
	Completion of new Ulm	*Marski*	Lange
	Th with only truly	*Faust II*	Goethe
	flexible modern audi-	*Wienerwald*	Horváth
	torium in Germany	*Purple Dust*	O'Casey
		Live Like Pigs	Arden
1967		*Soldaten*	Hochhuth
		Landshuter Erzählungen	Sperr
		Lusitanischer Popanz	Weiss
		Die Zimmerschlacht	Walser
		Nachr. aus der Provinz	Ziem
		Die Einladung	Ziem
		The Wars of the Roses	Shakespeare
		The Cherry Orchard	Chekhov
		The Silver Tassie	O'Casey
		Saved	Bond
1968	Demands for 'partici-	*Kaspar*	Handke
	pation' in management	*Toller*	Dorst
	of theatres	*Vietnam-Diskurs*	Weiss
	HANSGÜNTER	*Amphitryon*	Hacks
	HEYME goes to	*Magic Afternoon*	Bauer
	Cologne	*Biografie*	Frisch

110

Theatre	Director	Cast
Schsph Zurich	Hirschfeld	
Berliner Ens	Wekwerth/Palitzsch	Weigel
Dt Schsph Hamburg		
Ksp Munich		
Schiller-Th Werkstatt		
Schiller-Th Werkstatt		
Ulmer Th	Zadek	
Schsph Zurich	Horwitz	Knuth, Giehse
Schillerth Berlin		
Berliner Ens	Wekwerth/Tenschert	May
Shillerth Berlin	Kortner	Kammer, Held
Ksp Munich		
Dt Schsph Hamburg	Gründgens	Gründgens
Dt Th Berlin	Besson	
Freie Volksbn	Piscator	
Schsph Zurich		
Landesth Darmstadt		
Staatsth Stuttgart		
Schillerth Berlin	Swinarski	Schröder,
Aldwych Th London		Mosbacher
	Brook	Magee, Revill
Berliner Ens		
Freie Volksbn Berlin	Wekwerth/Tenschert	Schall, Weigel
Staatsth Stuttgart	Piscator	
Schaubn am H Ufer	Palitzsch	Mahnke
Freie Volksbn Berlin	Piscator	
Volksth Rostock	Perten	
Ksp Munich		
St Bn Frankfurt		
Dt Th Berlin	Besson	
Staatsth Stuttgart	Noelte	
Schsph Zurich		
Th am Turm Frankfurt	Peymann	
St Bn Oberhausen		
Th der Hansestadt Bremen		
Schillerth Berlin		
St Bn Frankfurt		
Schillerth Berlin		
Ksp Munich		
Berliner Ens	Simmgen	
Staatsth Stuttgart	Palitzsch	
Freie Volksbn Berlin		
Ksp Munich		
Schaubn am II Ufer	Paryla	
Ksp Munich	Kortner	
Schillerth Berlin		
Schlossparkth Berlin	Schweikart	
Staatsth Stuttgart	Palitzsch	
Staatsth Stuttgart	Zadek	
Wuppertal Bn	Zadek	
Ksp Munich	Stein	
Th am Turm Frankfurt	Peymann	
Staatsth Stuttgart	Palitzsch	
St Bn Frankfurt	Buckwitz	
Dt Th Göttingen		
Landesth Hanover		
Schsph Zurich		

Year	Event	Title	Author
		Hundsprozess/Herakles	Lange
		Philoktet	Müller
		Nachspiele	Wallraff
		Die Räuber	Schiller
1969	LIETZAU leaves	*Play Strindberg*	Dürrenmatt
	Residenzth Munich	*Gräfin von Rathenow*	Lange
		Mündel will Vormund sein	Handke
		Change	Bauer
		Davor	Grass
		Arbeitgeber	Kelling
		Torquato Tasso	Goethe
		Clavigo	Goethe
		Wallenstein	Schiller
		Krapp's Last Tape	Beckett
1970	Death of FRITZ	*Ritt über den Bodensee*	Handke
	KORTNER LIETZAU		
	takes over Schillerth	*Trotzki im Exil*	Weiss
	from BARLOG	*Martin Luther*	Forte
	Schaubn am Halles-	*Das Verhör von Habana*	Enzensberger
	chen Ufer reopens as	*Eiswichser*	Henkel
	a collective	*Guerillas*	Hochhuth
		Ein Fest für Boris	Bernhard
		Halbdeutsch	Mueller
		Die Mutter	Brecht
		The Cherry Orchard	Chekhov
1971		*Hölderlin*	Weiss
		Heimarbeit	Kroetz
		Bremer Freiheit	Fassbinder
		rozznjogd	Turrini
		Kinderspiel	Walser
		Münchner Freiheit	Sperr
		Peer Gynt	Ibsen
		Dance of Death	Strindberg
1972	PALITZSCH retires	*Stallerhof*	Kroetz
	from Staatsth	*Oberösterreich*	Kroetz
	Stuttgart	*Die neuen Leiden des W*	Plenzdorf
	Completion of Landesth	*Kleiner Mann, was nun?*	Dorst/Zadek
	Darmstadt	*Die Hebamme*	Hochhuth
	Death of HELENE	*Ignorant und der W.*	Bernhard
	WEIGEL	*Die Hypochonder*	Strauss
	PETER ZADEK	*Der Prinz von Homburg*	Kleist
	becomes *Intendant* in	*Fegefeuer in Ingolstadt*	Fleisser
	Bochum	*A Doll's House*	Ibsen
		Optimistic Tragedy	Wischnewski
1973		*Eiszeit*	Dorst
		Der Mitmacher	Dürrenmatt
		Zement	Müller
		Rheinpromenade	Mühl
		Frühlings Erwachen	Wedekind
		Richard III	Shakespeare
1974		*Die Unvernünftigen . . .*	Handke
		Macht der Gewohnheit	Bernhard
		Bacchae	Euripides
		King Lear	Shakespeare
1975	WERNER DÜGGE-	*Der Prozess*	Kafka/Weiss
	LIN retires from Basle	*Kellers Abend*	Muschg
	ARNO WÜSTEN-	*The Wild Duck*	Ibsen
	HÖFER leaves	*Miss Julie*	Strindberg
	Wuppertal Bn to take	*Waiting for Godot*	Beckett
	up post in Basle but		
	appointment not		
	confirmed		

Theatre	Director	Cast
Schaubn am H Ufer		
Residenzth Munich	Lietzau	
Landesth Castrop-Rauxel		
Residenzth Munich	Lietzau	Griem
Basler Th		
Bn der Stadt Cologne		
Th am Turm Frankfurt	Peymann	
Volksth Vienna		
Schillerth Berlin		
Landesth Castrop-Rauxel		
Th am Goetheplatz Bremen	Stein	Clever, Lampe
Dt Schsph Hamburg	Kortner	
Bn der Stadt Cologne	Heyme	
Schillerth Werkstatt	Beckett	Held
Schaubn am H Ufer	Peymann	Ganz, Clever, Lampe
Schsph Düsseldorf	Buckwitz	
Basler Th		
St Bn Essen		
Basler Th		
Staatsth Stuttgart		
Dt Schsph Hamburg	Peymann	
Ksp Munich		
Schaubn am H Ufer	Stein	Giehse
Residenzth Munich	Noelte	
Staatsth Stuttgart	Palitzsch	Roggisch
Ksp Munich	Siede	Schmidinger
Concordia Bremen		
Volksth Vienna		
Staatsth Stuttgart		
Schsph Düsseldorf		
Schaubn am H Ufer	Stein	Ganz
Schlossparkth Berlin	Noelte	Minetti
Dt Schsph Hamburg		
St Bn Heidelberg		
Landesth Halle	Schönemann	
Schsph Bochum	Zadek	
Ksp Munich		
Salzburg Festival		
Dt Schsph Hamburg		
Schaubn am H Ufer	Stein	
Schaubn am H Ufer	Stein	
Staatsth Stuttgart	Neuenfels	Roggisch
Schaubn am H Ufer	Stein	
Schsph Bochum	Zadek	Hasse
Schsph Zurich		
Berliner Ens	Berghaus	
Wuppertal Bn	Wüstenhöfer	
Staatsth Stuttgart	Palitzsch	
Dt Th Berlin	Wekwerth	
Schaubn am H Ufer	Stein	Ganz
Salzburg Festival	Dorn	Minetti
Schaubn am H Ufer	Grüber	Ganz
Schsph Bochum	Zadek	Mahnke
Bremen		
Basler Th	Düggelin	
Dt Schsph Hamburg	Zadek	
Berliner Ens	Berghaus	
Schillerth Berlin	Beckett	Wigger

Most frequently produced plays and playwrights 1964-74

These figures are based on theatre-programmes reported in *Theater heute*, which covers West Germany, Austria and Switzerland, but not East Germany. They refer to the number of productions per season of a given author or play and therefore only roughly reflect the number of performances or size of audiences (there is e.g. no distinction made between main auditorium and studio productions).

I lists the five most frequently produced dramatists of world theatre (excluding those listed under II).

II lists the five most frequently produced living German-language playwrights.

III lists the five most frequently produced contemporary plays in the German language (excluding Brecht).

In each case the number of productions appears after the name.

1964/65 Season

I			II		
1.	Shakespeare	67	1.	Kipphardt	24
2.	Brecht	39	2.	Dürrenmatt	20
3.	Schiller	34	3.	Weiss	8
4.	Anouilh ⎫ Shaw ⎭	33	4.	Frisch	7
			5.	Various authors	3

III 1. Kipphardt: *In Der Sache J. Robert Oppenheimer*   22
2. Dürrenmatt: *Der Besuch der alten Dame* ⎫
   Weiss: *Marat/Sade* ⎭   7
4. Dürrenmatt: *Die Ehe des Herrn Mississippi*   4
5. Dürrenmatt: *Die Physiker* ⎫
           Romulus der Grosse ⎭   3

1965/66 Season

I			II		
1.	Shakespeare	65	1.	Dürrenmatt	20
2.	Schiller	40	2.	Weiss	16
3.	Brecht	38	3.	Kipphardt	11
4.	Molière	34	4.	Frisch	9
5.	Anouilh	31	5.	Walser	6

III 1. Weiss: *Die Ermittlung* — 12
2. Kipphardt: *In der Sache J. Robert Oppenheimer* — 9
3. Dürrenmatt: *Romulus der Grosse* ⎫
        Der Meteor ⎭ — 5
5. Various plays — 4

1966/67 Season

I			II		
1.	Shakespeare	57	1.	Dürrenmatt	20
2.	Brecht	44	2.	Zuckmayer ⎫	9
3.	Schiller	31		Grass ⎭	
4.	Shaw	30	4.	Frisch ⎫	8
5.	Molière ⎫	29		Hacks ⎭	
	Anouilh ⎭				

III 1. Dürrenmatt: *Der Meteor* — 8
2. Zuckmayer: *Des Teufels General* — 7
3. Hacks: *Die Schlacht bei Lobositz* — 5
4. Frisch: *Don Juan oder Die Liebe zur Geometrie* — 4
   Dürrenmatt: *Romulus der Grosse*

1967/68 Season

I			II		
1.	Brecht	53	1.	Frisch	17
2.	Shakespeare	52	2.	Hochhuth	13
3.	Schiller	38	3.	Dürrenmatt	10
4.	Anouilh	21	4.	Handke	9
5.	Goethe	18	5.	Walser ⎫	7
				Ziem ⎭	

III 1. Hochhuth: *Soldaten* — 12
2. Frisch: *Biografie* — 10
3. Ziem: *Die Einladung* — 6
4. Zuckmayer: *Des Teufels General* — 5
5. Handke: *Publikumsbeschimpfung* ⎫ — 4
   Walser: *Der Abstecher* ⎭

1968/69 Season

I			II		
1.	Shakespeare	67	1.	Walser	23
2.	Brecht	44	2.	Handke	22
3.	Molière	32	3.	Hacks	12
4.	Schiller	25	4.	Dürrenmatt ⎫	11
5.	Anouilh	19		Frisch	
				Grass ⎭	

III 1. Walser: *Zimmerschlacht* — 20
2. Handke: *Kaspar* — 15
3. Hacks: *Amphitryon* — 11
4. Frisch: *Biografie* ⎫ — 8
   Hochhuth: *Soldaten* ⎭

1969/70 Season

I			II		
1.	Shakespeare	74	1.	Dürrenmatt	49
2.	Brecht	55	2.	Bauer	22

115

	3. Molière	34		3. Hacks	21
	4. Schiller	33		4. Frisch	16
	5. Anouilh	23		5. Grass	10

III	1. Dürrenmatt: *Play Strindberg*		27
	2. Bauer: *Magic Afternoon*		16
	3. Dürrenmatt: *König Johann*		14
	4. Hacks: *Amphitryon*		12
	5. Frisch: *Biografie* ⎫ Grass: *Davor* ⎭		9

1970/71 Season

I	1. Shakespeare	75	II	1. Dürrenmatt	37
	2. Brecht	62		2. Bauer	23
	3. Molière	24		3. Hacks	21
	4. Schiller	23		4. Hochhuth	15
	5. Goethe	18		5. Henkel	13

III	1. Dürrenmatt: *Play Strindberg*		23
	2. Henkel: *Eisenwichser*		13
	3. Bauer: *Magic Afternoon* ⎫ Hochhuth: *Guerillas* ⎭		12
	5. Hacks: *Amphitryon*		9

1971/72 Season

I	1. Shakespeare	57	II	1. Dürrenmatt	20
	2. Brecht	56		2. Weiss	14
	3. Molière	33		3. Forte ⎫ Henkel ⎭	12
	4. Schiller	18			
	5. Anouilh	17		5. Handke ⎫ Hacks ⎭	10

III	1. Forte: *Martin Luther* ⎫ Henkel: *Eisenwichser* ⎭		11
	3. Hochhuth: *Die Hebamme* Dürrenmatt: *Play Strindberg*		7
	5. Weiss: *Hölderlin*		6

1972/73 Season

I	1. Brecht	59	II	1. Kroetz	21
	2. Shakespeare	50		2. Dürrenmatt	17
	3. Molière	36		3. Hochhuth	16
	4. Schiller	22		4. Turrini	12
	5. Shaw	20		5. Fassbinder ⎫ Handke ⎬ Weiss ⎭	11

III	1. Hochhuth: *Die Hebamme*		15
	2. Fassbinder: *Bremer Freiheit*		10
	3. Turrini: *Der Tollste Tag*		9
	4. Bernhard: *Der Ignorant und der Wahnsinnige* ⎫ Forte: *Martin Luther* ⎬ Handke: *Kaspar* ⎪ Henkel: *Eisenwichser* ⎭		6

1973/74 Season

I				II			
	1.	Brecht	53		1.	Hacks	24
	2.	Shakespeare	52		2.	Kroetz	23
	3.	Molière	35		3.	Turrini	16
	4.	Schiller	23		4.	Handke	13
	5.	Goethe ⎱ Shaw ⎰	11		5.	Mühl	10

III 1. Hacks: *Adam und Eva* 15
    2. Kroetz: *Oberösterreich* ⎱
       Turrini: *Der tollste Tag* ⎰ 13
    4. Mühl: *Rheinpromenade* 10
    5. Plenzdorf: *Die neuen Leiden des jungen W.* 9

Ten-year period 1964–74

I				II			
	1.	Shakespeare	616		1.	Dürrenmatt	213
	2.	Brecht	503		2.	Hacks	111
	3.	Molière	303		3.	Handke	91
	4.	Schiller	287		4.	Frisch	87
	5.	Anouilh	210		5.	Weiss	77
					6.	Hochhuth	72
					7.	Walser	70
					8.	Bauer	51
					9.	Kroetz	50
					10.	Kipphardt	49

III 1. Dürrenmatt: *Play Strindberg* 62
    2. Hacks: *Amphitryon* 46
    3. Walser: *Zimmerschlacht* 41
    4. Bauer: *Magic Afternoon* ⎱
       Handke: *Kaspar* ⎰ 34
    6. Henkel: *Eisenwichser* ⎱
       Kipphardt: *In der Sache J. Robert Oppenheimer* ⎰ 33
    8. Frisch: *Biografie* 29
    9. Hochhuth: *Die Hebamme* 28
   10. Dürrenmatt: *König Johann* 27

Short bibliography

Major translations into English:

BAUER, Wolfgang: *All Change and other plays*, Calder & Boyars, London, 1973.

BORCHERT, Wolfgang: *The Man Outside*, Calder & Boyars, London, 1966.

DÜRRENMATT, Friedrich: *Four Plays* (*Romulus the Great, The Marriage of Mr. Mississippi, An Angel Comes to Babylon, The Physicists*,
 incl. Preface: *Problems of the Theatre*), Jonathan Cape, London, 1964.

The Meteor, Jonathan Cape, London, 1973.

The Physicists, Jonathan Cape, London, 1973.

Play Strindberg, Jonathan Cape, London, 1972.

The Visit, Jonathan Cape, London, 1962.

FRISCH, Max: *Andorra*, Methuen, London, 1964.

The Fire Raisers, Methuen, London, 1969.

Four Plays (*The Great Wall of China, Don Juan or The Love of Geometry, Philipp Hotz's Fury, Biography, a Game*) Methuen, London, 1969.

GRASS, Günter: *The Plebeians Rehearse the Uprising*, Penguin Books, Harmondsworth, 1972, (originally published by Secker & Warburg, 1967).

HANDKE, Peter: *Kaspar*, Methuen, London, 1972.

Offending the Audience and *Self-Accusation*, Methuen, London, 1971.

The Ride Across Lake Constance, Methuen, London, 1973.

They are Dying Out, Methuen, London, 1975.

HENKEL, Heinrich: *The Painters*, Davis-Poynter, London, 1974.

HOCHHUTH, Rolf: *The Deputy*, Grove Press, New York, 1964.

Soldiers, Grove Press, New York, 1968.

HOCHWÄLDER, Fritz: *The Strong Are Lonely*, Heinemann Educational, London, 1968.

KIPPHARDT, Heinar: *In The Matter of J. Robert Oppenheimer*, Methuen, London, 1967.

Postwar German Theatre, ed. and transl. Michael Benedikt and George E. Wellwarth, Macmillan, London, 1968. (Contains plays by Borchert, Dorst, Dürrenmatt, Frisch, Weiss, etc.)

SPERR, Martin: *Tales from Landshut*, Methuen, London, 1969.

WALSER, Martin: *Rabbit Race* and *Detour*, Calder & Boyars, London, 1971.

WEISS, Peter: *Discourse on Vietnam*, Calder & Boyars, London, 1971.
  The Investigation, Calder & Boyars, London, 1966.
  Marat/Sade, Calder & Boyars, London, 5th edn., 1969.
  Trotsky in Exile, Methuen, London, 1971.

ZUCKMAYER, Carl: *Des Teufels General*, Harrap, London, 1962.

Secondary literature in English:

BRECHT, Bertolt: *Brecht on Theatre*, Methuen, London, 1964.

COHN, Ruby: *Currents in Contemporary Drama*, Indiana Univ. Press, Bloomington & London, 1969.

GARTEN, H. F.: *Modern German Drama*, Methuen, London, 1959.

HAYMAN, Ronald (ed.): *The German Theatre*, Wolff, London, 1975.

HERN, Nicholas: *Peter Handke. Theatre and Anti-Theatre*, Wolff, London, 1970.

HILTON, Ian: *Peter Weiss. A Search for Affinities*, Wolff, London, 1970.

JENNY, Urs: *Dürrenmatt. A Study of His Plays*, Methuen, London, 1973.

SHAW, Leroy R. (ed.): *The German Theater Today. A Symposium*, Univ. of Texas, Austin, 1963.

SUBIOTTO, A. V.: *German Documentary Theatre*, Inaugural Lecture, Univ. of Birmingham, 1972.

THOMAS, R. Hinton, and Keith Bullivant: *Literature in Upheaval. West German Writers and the Challenge of the 1960s*, Manchester Univ. Press, Manchester, 1974.

WILLETT, John: *The Theatre of Bertolt Brecht. A Study from Eight Aspects*, Methuen, London, 1967.

Index

Aeschylus, 5

Ahlsen, Leopold, 2; *Am Galgen hängt die Liebe* (*Love Hangs on the Gallows*), 19; *Philemon und Baukis*, 19, 108

Albee, Edward, 101; *Who's Afraid of Virginia Woolf?*, 89, 90

Anouilh, Jean, 114, 115, 116, 117

Appen, Karl von. 10. 48. 80

Arden, John, 7, 102, 103; *Live Like Pigs*, 88, 102, 110, *Serjeant Musgrave's Dance*, 102

Aristophanes; *Peace*, 54, 110

Aristotle, 50

Artaud, Antonin, 10, 67

Ayckbourn, Alan, 5

Baierl, Helmut; *Frau Flinz*, 51, 110

Barlog, Boleslaw, 6, 8, 37, 106, 108, 112

Basle, 9, 59, 112; Basler Theater, 27, 28, 31, 54, 85, 98, 113
    Stadttheater, 23, 24, 107

Bauer, Wolfgang, 3, 93–4, 95, 104, 115, 116, 117
    Change (*All Change*), 8, 94, 112; *Gespenster* (*Ghosts*), 94; *Magic Afternoon*, 93–4, 110, 116, 117

Beaumarchais, Pierre Augustin Caron de; *The Barber of Seville*, 6; *The Marriage of Figaro*, 95

Becher, Johannes R.; *Winterschlacht* (*Winter Battle*), 51, 108

Becher, Ulrich; *Samba*, 108

Beckett, Samuel, 8, 25, 30, 32, 101, 112
    Krapp's Last Tape, 7, 112; *Waiting for Godot*, 30, 43, 112

Behan, Brendan; *The Hostage*, 110

Berghaus, Ruth, 9, 48, 113

Bergman, Ingmar, 66

Berlin, East, 3, 8, 45; College of Economics, 58;
    Deutsche Akademie der Künste, 80;
    Deutsches Theater, 6, 36, 45, 51, 52, 54, 64, 78, 106, 107, 109, 111, 113;
    Kammerspiele Deutsches Theater, 53, 107;
    Maxim-Gorki Theater, 58;
    Theater am Schiffbauerdamm, 6, 45, 108;
    Volksbühne, 52

Berlin, West, vii, 8, 59, 67;
    Deutsche Oper, 5;
    Freie Volksbühne, 9, 19, 75, 79, 80, 110, 111;
    Hebbeltheater, 107;
    Schaubühne am Halleschen Ufer, 7, 10, 11, 13, 31, 59, 65, 82, 88, 110, 111, 112, 113;
    Schillertheater, 8, 9, 12, 37. 40. 43, 66, 71, 108, 109, 110, 111, 112, 113:
    Schillertheater Werkstatt, 66, 71, 90, 111, 113,

Schlossparktheater, 6, 90, 106, 111, 113;
Tribüne, 22
Berliner Ensemble, 6, 7, 10, 12, 45–6, 48–51, 58, 62, 102, 106, 107, 108, 109, 111, 113
Berne; Ateliertheater, 33
Bernhard. Thomas; *Ein Fest für Boris* (*A Feast for Boris*), 112, *Der Ignorant und der Wahnsinnige* (*The Ignoramus and the Madman*), 112;
Die Macht der Gewohnheit (*The Power of Habit*), 112
Besson, Benno, 50, 54, 59, 62, 109, 111
Bielefeld (West Germany), 72
Bochum, 8, 10, 11, 14, 112; Schauspielhaus, 73, 113
Bond, Edward, 7; *Early Morning*, 102; *Saved*, 88, 102, 110
Borchert. Wolfgang, 3, 35–6, 101;
Das ist unser Manifest (*That Is Our Manifesto*), 36;
Draussen vor der Tür (*The Man Outside*), 1, 35–6, 106
Brandenburg (West Germany), 59
Brecht, Bertolt, 3, 5, 6, 8, 9, 10, 11, 12, 24, 32, 36, 38, 39, 43, 45–51, 53, 55, 56, 57, 58, 60, 62, 64, 66, 67, 73, 101, 102–3, 106, 107, 108, 114, 115, 116, 117
Antigone, 18, 46–8, 106; *Arturo Ui*, 10, 108;
Coriolan, 48–9, 110; *Don Juan*, 48;
Die Dreigroschenoper (*The Threepenny Opera*), 102;
Furcht und Elend des Dritten Reiches (*Fear and Misery in the Third Reich*), 91, 108;
Die Gesichte der Simone Machard (*The Visions of Simone Machard*), 108;
Die Gewehre der Frau Carrar (*Senora Carrar's Rifles*), 108;
Der gute Mensch von Sezuan (*The Good Women of Setzuan*), 46;
Die heilige Johanna der Schlachthöfe (*Saint Joan of the Stockyards*), 108;
Herr Puntila und sein Knecht Matti (*Mr. Puntila and His man Matti*), 46, 83, 106;
Der Hofmeister (*TheTutor*), 48, 106;
Der Kaukasische Kreidekreis (*The Caucasian Chalk Circle*), 51, 102, 108;
Kleines Organon für das Theater (*Small Organum for the Theatre*), 62, 106;
Leben des Galilei (*Life of Galileo*), 108;
Die Massnahme (*The Measures Taken*), 59;
Die Mutter (*The Mother*), 58, 112;
Mutter Courage (*Mother Courage*), 51, 102, 106;
Pauken und Trompeten (*The Recruiting Officer*), 48, 102;
Die Tage der Commune (*Days of the Commune*), 46, 50–1, 62, 72, 108, 110;
Urfaust, 48
Bregenz (Austria), 18, 108
Bremen, 10, 70; Concordia, 98, 113;
Theater der Freien Hansestadt, 91, 111;
Theater am Goetheplatz, 113
Brook, Peter, 6, 11, 26, 30, 49, 66, 67, 80, 82, 103, 111
Bruckner, Ferdinand; *Pyrrhus und Andromache*, 19
Brus, Günter, 100
Büchner, Georg; *Woyzeck*, 91, 92
Buckwitz Harry, 9, 39, 64, 82, 83, 106, 113
Busch, Ernst, 7, 109

Camus, Albert, 22
Castrop-Rauxel; Landestheater, 113
Celle; Scholosstheater, 22
Cheeseman, Peter, 103
Chekhov, Anton; *The Cherry Orchard*, 110, 113; *Three Sisters*, 110
Christie, Agatha; *Ten Little Niggers*, 43
Chur (Switzerland), 46, 107
Clever, Edith, 113
Cologne, 9, 10, 110; Bühnen der Stadt, 65, 66, 71, 101, 113
Constance; Deutsches Theater, 38

Darmstadt; Landestheater, 91, 95, 111, 112
Deichsel, Wolfgang; *bleiwe losse (Let It Be)*, 91
Dessau, Paul, 48
Deutsch, Ernst, 7
Dorn, Dieter, 113
Dorst, Tankred, vii, 3, 22, 72–3, 81, 102, 104;
   Eiszeit (Ice-Age), 15, 73, 112;
   Freiheit für Clemens (Freedom for Clemens), 72;
   Gesellschaft im Herbst (Autumn Party), 108;
   *Grosse Schmährede an der Stadtmauer (Great Denunciation by The City
      Wall)*, 110;
   Kleiner Mann, was nun? (Little Man—What Now?), 112;
   Die Kurve (The Bend), 108;
   Toller, 72–3, 110
Dortmund, Schauspiel, 95
Düggelin, Werner, 9, 112, 113
Durieux, Tilla, 7
Dürrenmatt, Friedrich, 3, 21–9, 34, 38, 40, 42, 43, 75, 101, 104, 114, 115, 116,
   117;
   Der Besuch der alten Dame (The Visit), 25–6, 39, 44, 103, 108, 114;
   Der Blinde (The Blind One), 23, 106;
   Die Ehe des Herrn Mississippi (The Marriage of Mr. Mississippi), 25, 29, 39,
      108, 114;
   Ein Engel kommt nach Babylon (An Angel Comes to Babylon), 23, 208;
   Es steht geschrieben (It Is Written), 23, 106;
   Herkules und der Stall des Augias (Hercules and the Augean Stable), 27, 44,
      110;
   König Johann (King John), 27, 116, 117;
   Der Meteor (The Meteor), 27–8, 110, 115;
   Der Mitmacher (The Conniver), 27, 112;
   Die Physiker (The Physicists), 26, 80, 101, 110, 114;
   Play Strindberg, 28–9, 54, 79, 101, 112, 116, 117;
   Porträt eines Planeten (Portrait of a Planet), 27;
   Romulus der Grosse (Romulus the Great), 24, 106, 114, 115;
   Theaterprobleme (Problems of the Theatre), 21, 108;
   Titus Andronicus, 27;
   Die Wiedertäufer (The Anabaptists), 23
Düsseldorf, 6, 9, 22; Schauspielhaus, 27, 83, 93, 108, 109, 113;
   Städtische Bühnen, 107

Eliot, Thomas Stearns, 47
Engel, Erich, 46, 80, 107, 109
Enzensberger, Hans-Magnus, 3, 101;
   Das Verhör von Habana (The Havana Hearing), 84–5, 87, 112
Erlangen Festival, 22
Essen; Städtische Bühnen, 84, 113
Euripides; *The Bacchae*, 11–12, 112

Farquhar, George; *The Recruiting Officer*, 48
Fassbinder, Rainer Werner, 89, 98, 116;
   Blut am Hals der Katze (Blood on the Cat's Neck), 98;
   Bremer Freiheit (Bremen Coffee), 98, 112, 116
Fehling, Jürgen, 109
Feuchtwanger, Lion; *Die Gesichte der Simone Machard (The Visions of
   Simone Machard)*, 108
Feydeau, Georges, 57
Fields, W. C., 11
Fleisser, Marieluise; *Fegefeuer in Ingolstadt (Purgatory in Ingolstadt)*, 88, 12;
   Pioniere in Ingolstadt (Pioneers in Ingolstadt), 88
Flickenschild, Elisabeth, 109
Floh de Cologne, 83
Forte, Dieter, 3, 104, 116; *Martin Luther und Thomas Münzer*, 85–6, 112, 116

Frankfurt, 7, 9, 10, 37, 64; Experimenta, 30;
  Städtische Bühnen, 13, 39, 43, 57, 64, 80, 82, 109, 110, 111;
  Theater-am-Turm (TAT), 9, 29, 30, 31, 111, 113
Frisch, Max, 3, 34–5, 37, 38–42, 43, 60, 75, 86, 101, 104, 114, 115, 116, 117;
  Als der Krieg zu Ende war (*When the War Was Over*), 40;
  Andorra, 26, 40–2, 103, 110;
  Biedermann und die Brandstifter (*The Fire-Raisers*), 27, 39–40, 103, 108;
  Biografie. Ein Spiel (*Biography. A Game*), 42, 101, 110, 115, 117;
  Die chinesische Mauer (*The Great Wall of China*), 39, 43, 106;
  Don Juan oder Die Liebe zur Geometrie (*Don Juan or The Love of Geometry*), 40, 108, 115;
  Graf Öderland (*Count Öderland*), 39, 108;
  Nun singen sie wieder (*Now They've Started Singing Again*), 34–5, 40, 106;
  Santa Cruz, 35;
  Tagebuch (*Diary*) *1946–49*, 34
Frost, Robert, 58

Ganz, Bruno, 7, 113
Gaskill, William, 63, 102
Gatti, Armand, 77
Giehse, Therese, 109, 111, 113
Giraudoux, Jean, 54
Gladkov, Fjodor, 59
Goethe, Johann Wolfgang von, 70, 115, 116, 117
  Clavigo, 112; *Faust I*, 7, 106;
  Faust II, 110;
  Die Leiden des jungen Werthers (*The Sorrows of Young Werther*), 99;
  Torquato Tasso, 122; *Urfaust*, 48
Goldoni, Carlo, 94
Göteborg, University of, 66
Göttingen; Deutsches Theater, 6, 9, 38, 54, 98, 107, 111
Grass, Günter, 3, 13, 22, 71–2, 73, 101, 102, 115, 116;
  Davor (*Beforehand*), 112, 116;
  Die bösen Köche (*The Wicked Cooks*), 71, 110;
  Onkel, Onkel (*Mister, Mister*), 71;
  Die Plebejer proben den Aufstand (*The Plebeians Rehearse the Uprising*),
    71–2, 103, 110
Graz; Schauspielhaus, 94
Greiz (East Germany), 62
Grieg, Nordahl; *The Defeat*, 50
Griem, Helmut, 113
Grotovski, Jerzy, 60
Grüber, Klaus Michael, 11, 113
Gründgens, Gustaf, 6, 7, 8, 19, 106, 107, 108, 109, 110, 111

Hacks, Peter, vii, 3, 12, 18, 24, 51–8, 60, 63, 73, 104, 115, 116, 117;
  Adam und Eva, 55, 117;
  Amphitryon, 54–5, 56, 57, 110, 115, 116, 117;
  Columbus, 52–3, 54, 56;
  Die Eröffnung des indischen Zeitalters (*The Introduction of the Indian Epoch*), 52–3, 108;
  Der Frieden (*Peace*), 54, 56, 110;
  Margarete in Aix, 54, 56;
  Moritz Tassow, 52, 56, 64;
  Der Müller von Sanssouci (*The Miller of Sanssouci*), 53–4, 56, 108;
  Omphale, 57;
  Die Schlacht bei Lobositz (*The Battle of Lobositz*), 53, 56, 57, 108, 115;
  Die Sorgen und die Macht (*Anxiety and Power*), 52, 108;
  Das Volksbuch von Herzog Ernst (*The Chap-Book of Duke Ernest*), 52
Hall, Peter, 102
Halle; Landestheater, 99, 113

Hamburg, 54; Deutsches Schauspielhaus, 8, 19, 65, 79, 94, 109, 111, 113;
   Deutsches Schauspielhaus Malersaal, 95;
   Kammerspiele, 35, 107;
   Opera House, 6;
   Thalia-Theater, 65
Handke, Peter, 3, 9, 13, 29–32, 75, 101, 104, 115, 116, 117;
   Hilferufe (*Cries for Help*), 30;
   Ich bin ein Bewohner des Elfenbeinturms (*I Am an Ivory-Tower Dweller*), 29;
   Kaspar, 30–1, 93, 104, 110, 116, 117;
   Der Mündel will Vormund sein (*My Foot, My Tutor*), 31, 112;
   Publikumsbeschimpfung (*Offending the Audience*), 22, 29, 31, 104, 110, 115;
   Quodlibet, 31;
   Der Ritt über den Bodensee (*The Ride Across Lake Constance*), 31–2, 112;
   Selbstbezichtigung (*Self-Accusation*), 30, 110;
   Die Unvernünftigen sterben aus (*They Are Dying Out*), 32, 112;
   Weissagung (*Prophecy*), 30
Hanover; Landestheater, 93, 111
Hare, David; *Fanshen*, 103
Hasse, O. E., 7, 113
Hatry, Michael; *Notstandsübung* (*Practising for a State of Emergency*), 83
Hauptmann, Gerhart, 95; *Die Atriden-Tetralogie* (*The Atridean Tetralogy*), 19
Hayman, Ronald, 102, 103
Hebbel, Friedrich; *Agnes Bernauer*, 96;
   Maria Magdalena, 96
Heidelberg; Städtische Bühnen, 96, 113
Heiseler, Bernt von; *Philoktet*, 19
Held, Martin, 7, 109, 111, 113
Henkel, Heinrich, 3, 118;
   Eisenwichser (*The Painters*), 98–9, 112, 116, 117
Heyme, Hansgünther, 9, 10, 103, 110, 113
Hildesheimer, Wolfgang, 3, 22, 102;
   Landschaft mit Figuren (*Landscape with Figures*), 22;
   Pastorale (*Pastoral*), 22, 108;
   Die Uhren (*The Clocks*), 22
Hilpert, Heinz, 6, 9, 37, 106, 107, 110
Hirschfeld, Kurt, 40, 46, 107, 111
Hobson, Harold, 94
Hochhuth, Rolf, 3, 13, 58, 75–8, 79, 80, 81, 82, 84, 85, 86, 115, 116, 117;
   Guerillas, 78, 112, 116;
   Die Hebamme (*The Midwife*), 98, 112, 116, 117;
   Soldaten (*Soldiers*), 75, 77–8, 103, 110, 115;
   Der Stellvertreter (*The Representative*), 37, 38, 75–7, 103, 110
Hochwälder, Fritz, 2, 16–18, 38;
   Donadieu, 17–18, 108;
   Das heilige Experiment (*The Strong Are Lonely*), 16, 103;
   Die Herberge (*The Inn*), 108;
   Der öffentliche Ankläger (*The Public Prosecutor*), 16, 18, 106
Hölderlin, Friedrich, 47
Hollmann, Hans, 59
Horváth, Ödön von, 3, 88–9, 97, 98;
   Geschichten aus dem Wienerwald (*Tales from the Vienna Woods*), 88, 91,
     110
   Kasimir und Karoline, 88, 110
Horwitz, Kurt, 107, 109, 111
Hunt, Albert, 8, 103

Ibsen, Henrik, 6, 8, 32;
   A Doll's House, 112;
   Hedda Gabler, 29;
   Peer Gynt 7, 112;
   The Wild Duck, 112
Ionesco, Eugène, 89; *The Bald Prima-Donna*, 25: *The Rhinoceroses*, 6, 22, 108

Jahnn, Hans Henny, 2;
    Der staubige Regenbogen (*The Dusty Rainbow*), 80;
    Thomas Chatterton, 19–20, 108
Jaspers, Karl; *Die Atombombe und die Zukunft des Menschen* (*The Atom-Bomb and the Future of Man*), 79
Joint Stock Company, 8, 103
Joyce, James, 47

Kafka, Franz, 43, 66; *Der Prozess* (*The Trial*), 112
Kammer, Klaus, 111
Karl-Marx-Stadt (East Germany), 50, 108
Kayser, Professor Karl, 61
Keaton, Buster, 11, 31
Kelling, Gerhard; *Arbeitgeber* (*Employers*), 112
Kierkegaard, Søren, 96
Kipphardt, Heinar, 3, 12, 78–80, 82, 86, 114, 117;
    Der Hund des Generals (*The General's Dog*), 110;
    In der Sache J. Robert Oppenheimer (*In the Matter of J. Robert Oppenheimer*), 79–80, 84, 103, 110, 114, 115, 117;
    Joel Brand, 79, 110;
    Shakespeare dringend gesucht (*Wanted Urgently: Shakespeare*), 108
Kleist, Heinrich von, 54;
    Die Marquise von O. (*The Marchioness of O.*), 65;
    Der Prinz von Homburg (*The Prince of Homburg*), 112
Knuth, Gustav, 107, 109, 111
Kortner, Fritz, 9, 89, 107, 111, 113
Kroetz, Franz Xaver, vii, 3, 89, 95–8, 99, 104, 116, 117;
    Agnes Bernauer, 96;
    Dolomitenstadt Lienz (*Lienz, Town in the Dolomites*), 96;
    Heimarbeit (*Home-Worker*), 95, 112;
    Maria Magdalena, 96;
    Oberösterreich (*Morecambe*), 96–8, 112, 119;
    Stallerhof (*Staller Farm*), 95–6, 98, 112;
    Wildwechsel (*Wild Animals Crossing*), 95;
    Wunschkonzert (*Request Programme*), 96

Labiche, Eugène, 10
Lampe, Jutta, 7, 113
Lange, Hartmut, 3, 64–5, 74;
    Die Gräfin von Rathenow (*The Countess of Rathenow*), 12, 65, 112;
    Herakles, 65, 112;
    Hundsprozess (*Dogs' Trial*), 65, 112;
    Marski, 64, 110;
    Trotzki in Coyoacan, 65
Leipzig; Karl Marx University, 59; Städtische Theater, 58, 190
Lenz, Jakob Michael Reinhold; *Der Hofmeister* (*The Tutor*), 48, 106
Lenz, Siegfried, 3, 101;
    Zeit der Schuldlosen (*Time of the Guiltless*), 65–6, 110
Lessing, Gotthold Ephraim;
    Nathan der Weise (*Nathan the Wise*), 106
Lietzau, Hans, 108, 110, 112, 113
Littlewood, Joan, 82
London, 16, 66, 102, 108;
    Aldwych Theatre, 8, 80, 111;
    Half Moon Theatre, 8;
    National Theatre, 12;
    Royal Court Theatre, 63;
    West End, 7, 65, 102
Löbeck; Bühnen der Hansestadt, 109

Magee, Patrick, 111
Mahnke, Hans, 111, 113
Mannheim; Nationaltheater, 108, 109

Marx Brothers, The, 11
Matusche, Alfred; *Die Dorfstrasse (The Village-Street)*, 108
May, Gisela, 111
Mexico; Heinrich Heine Club, 51
Meyer, Conrad, 17
Michelsen, Hans Günter, 22: *Helm*, 43–4, 110
Minetti, Bernhard, 113
Minks, Wilfried, 10
Molière, 24, 54, 114, 115, 116, 117
    Don Juan, 48
Mosbacher, Peter, 111
Mueller, Harald, 63; *Der grosse Wolf (Big Wolf)*, 63;
    Halbdeutsch (Half German), 112
Mühl, Karl Otto, 119;
    Rheinpromenade (Promenade by the Rhine), 98, 112, 117
Mühl, Otto, 100
Müller, Armin, 63
Müller, Heiner, 3, 58–60, 63, 73;
    Der Bau (The Building-Site), 58, 59;
    Die Korrektur (The Correction), 58;
    Der Lohndrücker (Lowering the Wages), 58, 59, 108;
    Macbeth, 59–60;
    Philoktet (Philoctetes), 59, 112;
    Die Umsiedlerin (Change of Residence), 58, 59;
    Zement (Cement), 58, 59, 112
Munich, vii; antiteater, 98;
    Kammerspiele, 9, 19, 22, 23, 25, 43, 63, 79, 88, 89, 92, 94, 95, 98, 109, 111, 113
    Residenztheater, 59, 110, 112, 113
Muschg, Adolf; *Kellers Abend (Keller's Evening)*, 112

Neher, Casper, 10, 46, 107, 110
Neuenfels, Hans, 113
New York (Broadway), 7, 16, 103
Nitsch, Herbert, 100
Noelte, Rudolf, 111, 113
Nuremberg; Städtische Bühnen, 98

Oberhausen; Städtische Bühnen, 30, 111
O'Casey, Sean; *Purple Dust*, 110; *The Silver Tassie*, 110
Offenbach, Jacques, 6
Olivier, Laurence, 7
Osborne, John, 88;
    The Entertainer, 102;
    Look Back in Anger, 102;
    Luther, 85, 102

Palitzsch, Peter, 9, 43, 48, 51, 64, 103, 108, 109, 110, 111, 112, 113
Paris, 16, 30, 66; Théâtre des Nations, 108
Paryla, Karl, 82, 111
Perten, Hanns Anselm, 70, 111
Peymann, Claus, 29, 30, 31, 111, 113
Pinter, Harold, 32, 88, 90, 98, 101;
    The Caretaker, 108;
    The Dumb Waiter, 7, 10, 108;
    Revue Sketches, 90
Pirandello, Luigi, 42
Piscator, Erwin, 7, 9, 10, 19, 75, 76, 78, 79, 80, 108, 109, 110, 111
Planchon, Roger, 66, 82, 103
Plautus, 54
Plenzdorf, Ulrich, 3, 58, 104;
    Die neuen Leiden des jungen W (The New Sorrows of Young W), 61, 99, 117
Pound, Ezra, 47

Racine, Jean, 19
Recklinghausen; Ruhr Festival, 83
Reinhardt, Max, 8
Revill, Clive, 111
Roggisch, Peter, 113
Rossini, Gioacchino Antonio; *The Barber of Seville*, 6
Rostock, 70; Volkstheater, 80, 111
Royal Shakespeare Company, 80

Salzburg Festival, 114
Sartre, Jean-Paul; *The Flies*, 106
Saxe-Meiningen, Duke of, 7
Schall, Ekkehard, 10, 48, 49, 109, 111
Schalla, Hans, 8
Scheller, Bernhard, 59
Schiller, Friedrich, 6, 16, 18, 21, 24, 26, 70, 76, 114, 115, 116, 117;
    Don Carlos, 10, 15, 106, 110; *Maria Stuart*, 11, 108;
    Die Räuber (*The Robbers*), 112;
    Wallenstein, 112
Schleef, Einar, 115
Schmidinger, Walter, 113
Schneider, Reinhold; *Der grosse Verzicht* (*The Great Renunciation*), 18, 108
Schönemann, Horst, 99, 113
Schröder, Ernst, 111
Schumacher, Ernst; *Die Versuchung des Forschers* (*The Temptation of a Research Scientist*), 80
Schwab, Gustav, 31
Schwartz, Jewgenij; *Der Drache* (*The Dragon*), 110
Schweikart, Hans, 9, 25, 90, 109, 111
Senftenberg (East Germany), 52, 109
Shakespeare, William, 6, 11, 24, 58, 60, 114, 115, 116, 117;
    Coriolanus, 48–9, 110;
    King John, 27;
    King Lear, 11, 112;
    Macbeth, 59;
    The Merchant of Venice, 15;
    A Midsummer Night's Dream, 11;
    Richard III, 112;
    Romeo and Juliet, 92;
    Titus Andronicus, 27;
    The Wars of the Roses, 110
Shaw, George Bernard, 6, 114, 115, 116, 117;
    Captain Brassbound's Conversion, 7, 106
Siede, Horst, 113
Simmgen, Hans Georg, 111
Sommer, Harald; *A unhamlich schtorka obgong* (*A Gruesomely Strong Exit*), 93
Sophocles, 8, 19;
    Antigone, 40, 44, 47, 106;
    King Oedipus, 106
Sperr, Martin, 3, 91–3, 95;
    Jagdszenen aus Niederbayern (*Hunting Scenes from Lower Bavaria*, 91–2, 93, 110;
    Landshuter Erzählungen (*Tales from Landshut*), 92–3, 110;
    Müncher Freiheit (*Munich Freedom*), 93, 112
Stafford-Clark, Max, 102
Stanislavski, Konstantin, 8, 102
Steckel, Leonard, 39, 46, 107, 109
Stein, Peter, 10, 88, 113
Stifter, Adalbert, 27
Stockholm, 30, 66; Scala-Teatern, 82; Studio, 66
Stoke-on-Trent; Victoria Theatre, 103
Strauss, Botho; *Die Hypochonder* (*The Hypochondriacs*), 93, 112

Strehler, Giorgio, 103
Strindberg, August, 66;
  Dance of Death, 28–9, 101, 112;
  Miss Julie, 112
Strittmatter, Erwin; *Katzgraben*, 51, 108
Stroux, Karl Heinz, 9, 22, 108, 109
Stuttgart, 64; Neues Theater, 16, 107;
  Staatstheater, 43, 70, 72, 78, 88, 110, 111, 113
Swinarski, Konrad, 67, 111
Synge, John Millington, 58; *The Playboy of the Western World*, 63

Tenschert, Joachim, 46, 48, 50, 111
Theatermanufaktur, 83
Tolstoy, Count Leo; *War and Peace*, 78, 108
Tübingen; Landestheater (LTT), 9
Turrini, Peter, 98, 118, 119;
  Rozznjogd (Rat Hunt), 94, 112;
  Sauschlachten (Slaughter of the Pigs), 94;
  Der tollste Tag (The Most Crazy Day), 116, 117
Tynan, Kenneth, 103

Ulm; Hochschule für Gestaltung, 83;
  Podiumtheater, 11; Ulmer Theater, 111

Verdi, Giuseppe, 5
Vienna; Burgtheater, 6, 10, 17, 18, 106, 109;
  Theater am Belvedere, 66; Theater in der Josefstadt, 109;
  Volkstheater, 94, 113
Vietta, Egon; *Iphigenie in Amerika*, 19
Voltaire, François-Marie Arouet de; *Candide*, 27

Wagner, Richard, 10
Wallraff, Günter; *Nachspiele (Games That Followed)*, 83, 112
Walser, Martin, 3, 42–3, 81, 89, 101, 114, 115, 117;
  Der Abstecher (The Detour), 89, 110, 115;
  Eiche und Angora (Rabbit Race), 42–3, 73, 110;
  Ein Kinderspiel (Child's Play), 43, 112;
  Realismus X, 42;
  Der schwarze Schwan (The Black Swan), 43, 101, 110;
  Überlebensgross Her Krott (Herr Krott Larger Than Life), 110;
  Die Zimmerschlacht (Home-Front), 43, 89–90, 110, 115
Wälterlin, Oskar, 109
Wedekind, Frank; *Frühlings Erwachen (Spring Awakening)*, 112
Weigel, Helene, 7, 45, 46, 107, 109, 112
Weisenborn, Günther; *Die Illegalen (Outside the Law)*, 106
Weiss, Peter, 3, 66–71, 72, 73, 74, 75, 80–4, 86, 101, 104, 114, 116, 117;
  Die Ermittlung (The Investigation), 1, 2, 34, 80–2, 83, 103, 110, 115;
  Gesang vom Lusitanischen Popanz (Song of the Lusitanian Bogey), 82–3, 110;
  Hölderlin, 70–1, 101, 112, 116;
  Marat/Sade, 30, 66–70, 81, 101, 103, 110, 114;
  Nacht mit Gästen (Night with Guests), 66;
  Der Prozess (The Trial), 70, 112;
  Trotzki im Exil (Trotsky in Exile), 83–4, 112;
  Der Turm (The Tower), 66;
  Die Versicherung (The Insurance), 66;
  Vietnam-Diskurs (Vietnam-Discourse), 82–3, 110
Wekwerth, Manfred, 46, 48, 49, 50, 51, 80, 103, 108, 109, 111, 113;
Wesker, Arnold, 88
Wiens, Wolfgang, 31
Wigger, Stefan, 113
Wilder, Thornton; *Our Town*, 25;
  The Skin of Our Teeth, 25, 106

Williams, Tennessee, 61
Wischnewski, Wsewolod; *Optimistic Tragedy*, 112
Wittlinger, Karl; *Kennen Sie die Milchstrasse? (Do You Know the Milky Way?)*, 101, 103
Wolfit, Donald, 8
Wünsche, Konrad; *Der Unbelehrbare (The Unteachable One)*, 110
Wuppertal, 9; Bühnen, 111; Schauspielhaus, 110
Württemberg; Landesbühne, 14
Wüstenhöfer, Arno, 9, 112, 113

Zadek, Peter, 8, 9, 11, 14, 15, 73, 111, 112, 113
Ziem, Jochen, 3, 89, 90–1, 93, 99, 115;
    Die Einladung (The Invitation), 90, 110, 115;
    Nachrichten aus der Provinz (News from the Provinces), 90–1, 110
Zuckmayer, Carl, 3, 12, 36–8, 43, 115;
    Barbara Blomberg, 38;
    Der Gesang im Feuerofen (Song of the Furnace), 38, 106;
    Der Hauptmann von Köpenick (The Captain of Köpenick), 37;
    Das kalte Licht (The Cold Light), 79, 108;
    Des Teufels General (The Devil's General), 6, 37–8, 73, 86, 106, 115;
    Ulla Winblad, 38
Zurich, 25; Schauspielhaus, 6, 9, 23, 25, 26, 27, 34, 37, 39, 40, 42, 46, 98, 107, 109, 111, 113
    Theater am Neumarkt, 32